When Your Child Has Been Molested

When Your Child Has Been Molested

A Parent's Guide to Healing and Recovery

KATHRYN B. HAGANS
JOYCE CASE

Jossey-Bass Publishers • San Francisco

FIRST JOSSEY-BASS EDITION PUBLISHED IN 1998.
THIS BOOK WAS ORIGINALLY PUBLISHED BY LEXINGTON BOOKS.

Substantial discounts on bulk quantities of Jossey-Bass books are available to corporations, professional associations, and other organizations. For details and discount information, contact the special sales department at Jossey-Bass Inc., Publishers (415) 433-1740; Fax (800) 605-2665.

For sales outside the United States, please contact your local Simon & Schuster International Office.

Jossey-Bass Web address: http://www.josseybass.com

Printed in the United States of America on acid-free paper.

Library of Congress Cataloging-in-Publication Data

Brohl, Kathryn.
   When your child has been molested : a parent's guide to healing and recovery / Kathryn B. Hagans, Joyce Case.
     p. cm.
   Originally published: Lexington, Mass. : Lexington Books, © 1988.
   Includes index.
   ISBN 0-7879-4073-9 (pbk.)
   1. Child sexual abuse—United States. 2. Sexually abused children—United States—Psychology. 3. Child sexual abuse—Investigation—United States. 4. Sexually abused children—United States—Family relationships. 5. Sexually abused children—Counseling of—United States. I. Case, Joyce. II. Title.
HQ72.U53H33 1998
362.76—dc21
                                           97-38475
                                             CIP

HB Printing   10 9 8 7 6
PB Printing   10

This book is offered, with love, to every family whose life has been temporarily devastated by a child's sexual molestation. It is dedicated, with great hope, to the healing of those courageous children and their grieving families.

Contents

Reality Checks

Acknowledgments

W E all rely on other people in our everyday professional and private lives, but a project such as this brings into focus how much wonderful support and input others actually provide.

We wish to acknowledge (alphabetically) the unselfish sharing of the following people of their experience, expertise, time, and interest to help make this project successful: RaiEtte Avael, Florida Health and Rehabilitative Services, Fort Myers; Beverly Blow, Florida Assistant State Attorney, Fort Myers; Mary Sanders-Damroth, M.A.; Janet DeFranchesco, M.A., Bonita Middle School instructor; Becky Gunder, Case Coordinator, CPT Lee County; Roger Gunder, M.S., Sexual Abuse Treatment Program Therapist, Fort Myers; Diane Goldberg, M.S.W.; Dennis Harrison, Ph.D., Sexual Abuse Treatment Consultant; Jonellen Heckler, author; Jeffrey A. Kuhn, National Council of Juvenile and Family Court Judges; Linda Lanier, Planned Parenthood, Jacksonville; Michael Lanier, M.A., Florida State Consultant for Sexual Abuse Treatment Programs; Jill Turner, Child Protection Team of Lee County, Director; The Honorable Hugh Starnes, Family Court Judge, Lee County; Major Don Schmidt, Lee County Sheriff's Department; Deborah Silver, Ph.D., Consulting Psychologist, Sexual Abuse Treatment Program of Collier and Lee Counties; and Robert Silver, Ph.D.

As single parents with other full-time professional obligations, we wish to offer printed hugs to our daughters Susie Sharp and Angie Case, for their patience with us while we filled some of our "mothering" time with book writing. It was wonderful, too, that they never doubted that we could "do it!"

We want to encourage others who might be thinking about producing a book they feel is badly needed: it can be done! And two friends *can* begin a book and finish it—many months later—*still* friends.

Introduction

Putting the Pieces Back Together

THIS book is designed to help you and your family get through the difficult time after you suspect or become aware of the molestation of your child. Our goal is to aid you in rebuilding your family unit after the trauma a molestation can cause. Unfortunately, family members often feel very alone and draw apart during and after such a crisis.

The legal steps and the psychological stresses following the report of a sexual molestation are sometimes complicated and lengthy. The information given here is not intended to frighten you as a parent or guardian, nor to alarm your child. We want to offer you information, guidance, and support. By knowing what to expect as you work with the necessary authorities, you can lessen your anxieties, make your cooperation with the various agencies productive, and reduce the additional frustrations that arise if you hold unrealistic expectations.

"Reality Checks" are provided throughout this book to help you and your family compare your experiences, feelings, knowledge, and behaviors against norms compiled from facts and findings in the field of sexual abuse of children. They are not here to tell you that what you're doing, thinking, or feeling is "wrong." They will, instead, usually offer you reassurance that your feelings are shared by many others who have had to face this experience. Some Reality Checks may suggest more productive ways of dealing with or working through a situation; others will help you and your family dispel some commonly held misinformation about sexual molestation.

We have provided a glossary of terms for you near the end of the book. In all professions and areas of interest, some common words take on specialized meanings, familiar to the people who use them daily in their work, but confusing to others. As you deal with various professionals, don't ever hesitate to ask exactly what they mean by a particular word. Don't feel that they think you "should know." They are simply using words so common in their work that they sometimes forget the terms may be unfamiliar to you. As an example, "molest" is listed in most dictionaries as only a verb—an action word—with definitions such as "to accost and harass sexually." Yet professionals in the field of sexual abuse treatment commonly use it also as a noun—the name for what happened: the molest. So you may hear it used both ways.

You cannot cooperate fully or follow instructions precisely if you don't understand what is being requested. You also cannot tell someone whether you feel they are right or wrong about something they are saying unless you understand them clearly.

You may find it helpful to read through the entire glossary now, so you will feel more comfortable with the terms as you come across them in the book.

For less repetitive reading, we have deliberately avoided using the more legally correct term "*alleged*" with offender and molester, even when referring to a suspected person before he or she has been found guilty in court.

Scott and the Thompson family, whose progress is followed throughout the book, are composites of many children and many families who have been through the experience of a molestation. It would not be fair, even with permission, to open an actual family to such scrutiny in a crisis situation. They are "real" in that they represent the feelings and behaviors common to many such victims and families and are drawn from working with hundreds of families in sexual abuse situations.

If you have progressed to some middle-stage of the investigative or legal process when you read this, don't be discouraged by the things you have already done very differently from what is suggested here. If it is clear that what is recommended would have been better and there is some way to change what you have done, do it. If not, go on from wherever you are now—comforted by knowing you did your best. Give yourself permission to let go of any mistakes you feel you made, and use this book and all available resources to make future decisions with which you will be comfortable.

Families need outside help when a tragedy such as molestation occurs. This book will help, but you will need more. Be sure to use the in-person assistance available from agencies and organizations in your area who regularly serve people coping with this devastating experience. The more you use all of the available recovery resources, the more quickly you and your family can feel whole and healthy again.

1

Learning That Your Child Has Been Molested

JANET and Bill Thompson recently learned that their son Scott has been sexually molested. Friendly, intelligent and eager to please, nine-year-old Scott is well liked. This year he played Tom Sawyer in the class play and, with his reddish hair and freckles, he looked the part. He loves almost anything that can be done outside, and often builds tree houses and forts with neighborhood kids.

The Thompsons are overwhelmed by the thought that someone could violate the child they so lovingly nurtured and protected. How could this have happened? How had they failed him? Did he believe them when they said they'd see that nothing like this would ever happen to him again? Was it a realistic promise? Were their feelings realistic? How could they protect their seven-year-old Beth? Had anything ever happened to Brad, their sixteen-year-old son, that he never told them?

The Thompsons had always spent a great deal of time with Scott and their other children, and had enrolled them in activities they thought would make them feel good about themselves. One of Scott's activities was a boys' camping club, much like one Bill remembered fondly from his youth. During his first two years as a member, Scott had expressed the same enthusiasm for the club's members and outdoor activities as

Bill recalled feeling, but recently his interest had dwindled. He would absently forget meeting times, or withdraw to his room and say he didn't feel like going, or that he was getting too old for "that camping stuff."

A few days ago, while Bill and Scott were repainting the family's fishing boat, Scott asked casually what homosexuals do. Bill explained vaguely, somewhat unsure of what Scott really wanted to know. Scott said the guys in the camping club thought their leader, Mr. Webster, "was one."

Bill's mind raced nervously, but he tried to sound calm as he asked Scott why the kids believed that. Embarrassed and looking away, Scott said sometimes Mr. Webster said funny things to him when they were alone, things that made his stomach do sick flip-flops. Bill quietly encouraged Scott to explain, and kept on painting the boat with studied concentration.

Scott kept painting, too, and said Mr. Webster had told him how much he liked to see the boys when they had their clothes off because they looked so much more comfortable. He said Mr. Webster sometimes stared at him for a long time, and sometimes Mr. Webster's hand brushed across his crotch when they were standing near each other, or were involved in group activities.

Scott, who was embarrassed and overwhelmed by such remarks and actions from an authority figure, had chosen to withdraw from contact with Webster by not going to club meetings. Bewildered by the confusing emotions of growing up, Scott feared Webster's comments and actions labeled him a homosexual, too.

Bill told Scott that no one had the right to touch him in ways that made him feel uncomfortable, and that Webster should not have said and done those things.

With Scott's information, Bill and Janet began discreetly asking other club members' parents if they had observed or heard anything about Mr. Webster inappropriately touching or talking to their sons. It was soon evident that other boys also felt uncomfortable with him. Sometimes reluctantly and sometimes with relief at being able to share the information, several divulged the same types of experiences. After a few days, Scott finally told that Webster had fondled him and asked him to engage in mutual masturbation.

Who Molests Children?

Janet and Bill were particularly disturbed to think that a person pretending to care so much about young people would take advantage of a position of trust. How could they ever trust outsiders again? How could Scott be protected from the same type of abuse by someone else? How could they decide which situations were safe and which were not? Or could they? They couldn't lock Scott in a closet or even unreasonably restrict his activities and still offer him a normal childhood.

Certainly most people who work with children do it for the right reasons. But the reality is that people who molest children often place themselves in positions in which they have extended contact with children.

The facts are that many sex offenders know their victims, and sexual molestation may occur in a progression of actions over a period of time, or happen in a single occurrence when the offender takes advantage of a unique opportunity or situation.

To help you and your family clarify your thinking on the types of people who are child molesters, Reality Check Number 1 details current findings about molestations. Some of the facts given are from *Sexual Assault of Children and Adolescents* by Burgess, Groth, Holmstrom, and Sgroi. This information is not meant to build hysteria among parents or children, only to build a factual base for your feelings about sexual abuse and abusers.

Reality Check Number 1:
What Are Some of the Facts about Sexual Abuse and Abusers?

✔ Intercourse is not necessary for the incident to constitute sexual abuse. (See legal definition in chapter 3.)

✔ Children do not seduce adults.

✔ Sexual molestation has historically occurred, and continues to occur, in all types of societies worldwide.

✔ Molestation behavior is not prompted by a physical illness.

✔ Most people are not insane when they molest children. Data indicate less than 5 percent of molesters show clinical evidence of psychosis (loss of contact with reality) at the time of their offenses.

✔ There is no one valid profile for all sexual molesters. All ages, all economic groups, all levels of intelligence, all races, and all religions are represented in the backgrounds of people who have molested children.

✔ Child molesters are single and married, heterosexual and homosexual, male and female.

✔ Frequently, the molesters were victims of molestation.

✔ The majority of people who sexually abuse children know their victims.

✔ Therapists relate that most sexual offenders do not molest just one time. Reports indicate that one molester can molest many times before being apprehended.

✔ The use of alcohol or drugs, as it relates to the sexual offender, should not minimize or justify the sexual offense.

✔ Molestations by young offenders (even the very young) should be treated with the same concern and care as those by older offenders.

✔ Any child can be victimized: a friendly, talkative child as well as a shy and withdrawn child, smart children and slow children.

Types of Molesters

To be able to believe your child's reality or truth, it is helpful to be aware of the types of molesters as defined by Dr. Nicholas Groth. He classifies child molesters into two groups:

1. Regressed molesters, usually capable of being helped by a community-based (unconfined) treatment program, are those individuals who clearly have a sexual orientation toward people near their own age. Their molestation of a child is a departure from their usual sex patterns, often occurring under stress.

2. Fixated molesters, who have a primary sex orientation toward children, prefer children for sex partners because they feel more comfortable with them. They often prefer prepubescent children (those who have not yet developed pubic hair, breasts, and other signs of adolescence). Often these people only respond to treatment when it is administered in a setting in which they are confined.

Therapists are finding that molesters in both groups, when granted immunity from prosecution, will often admit to having molested children beginning at an earlier age than when finally apprehended, and to molesting many more children than initially reported.

People who molest children often appear "normal." They have families and jobs. They include, but are certainly not limited to, physicians, police officers, choir directors, letter carriers, coaches, construction workers, teachers, funeral directors, youth group leaders, ministers—and people in every other profession. They are family friends and neighbors with an extensive self-rationale (justification) for their molestations. They are not somewhere "out there;" they are among us.

Frequently molesters were victims of molestation. Experts find their outward personalities often hide despair and self-loathing. Sex offenders have not learned positive ways of dealing with stress. Often they are also abusers of drugs and alcohol, and may be physically abusive as well as being child molesters. Many times their relationships with their "significant others" (people playing important roles in their personal lives) are troubled.

Bill and Janet were grateful that Scott had come to them to talk about the molestation. They knew how embarrassed and worried their child must have felt explaining the incidents. Though Bill learned about the experience directly from his child, many times parents learn about their child's abuse from other sources.

One of the most shocking ways to learn about an abuse is to witness the act, or to hear directly from someone else who saw the incident. One mother reports being immobilized and unable to react when she walked into the room where a neighbor girl, considerably older than her child, was performing oral sex on her daughter. Another parent says she had difficulty believing her nephew when he reported watching a sixteen-year-old male babysitter kissing her five-year-old daughter on the mouth.

Often molested children will report first to someone they feel will not overreact to the information. Frequently they first report that they were molested or are being molested when they get into day care or school. This may be the first that they become aware that what has happened is not normal adult/child behavior.

The child may mention the molestation casually during a play activity, seeking to have his or her feeling confirmed that what happened was not "right." Unusual behavior may be an indirect way that a child reports an abuse. If so, he or she may only reveal the experience after being questioned about it directly.

An astute teacher may spot indications of an abuse in a child's drawings or writings. Day-care workers may observe extreme behaviors in a child. These indications may lead them to question the child about what is worrying him or her. A child's playmates may express a worry about their friend to their own parents. A favorite relative may be told the child's story during a casual conversation they have together. During the course of a routine physical examination, a child may divulge an abuse after a doctor questions her or him about an abrasion in the genital area.

It is not uncommon for child protection agencies to receive the first report of a molestation from a victim's extended family member, a school official, teacher, day-care worker, friend, or the parents of another child.

Often parents feel hurt that their child did not initially tell them. One mother explained, "I felt that my parenting of Laurie was lacking because she didn't let me know first. I felt really guilty." Guilt is a normal feeling in response to hearing about your child's experience. You may feel you "should have been there" or "should have been able to prevent it." You may also feel guilt masked by anger. Don't allow your anger or hurt to stand in the way of good *future* communication with your child, even if he or she did not mention the abuse to you first.

Often children do not tell their parents because they are afraid of parents' reactions; they don't want to burden their parents; they fear being disbelieved; they fear being considered "crazy;" or they're afraid they'll be sent away. These are logical fears for children, based on their lack of knowledge, and do not necessarily reflect their parents' actual ability to deal properly with the information.

However you became aware of the molestation, give your child the support and love so desperately needed through the legal process and recovery period that must follow.

2

The Importance of Reporting the Abuse and What Happens Next

JANET hung up the phone. She had just reported the sexual molestation of Scott to the police. She cried.

Janet felt she had taken a risk when she phoned the police department. Having no experience or preparation for this experience, she had little idea of what she and her family were facing. Everyone in the family was very unsure of how to feel and what to expect.

Janet calmed herself; then she and Bill explained to Scott that the call was necessary to protect him and the other boys from further abuse. (Chapter 3 discusses what to say to your child to relieve his or her fears when a report is made.)

Though she did not voice her fears to Scott, Janet was nearly as worried about what Scott would have to go through during the investigation that would follow as she was about the frightening incidents he had already experienced. What would he be expected to explain? What charges would he have to make before the abuser could be prosecuted? How many people would Scott have to talk with? How long would the process take? Would they arrest Mr. Webster immediately? What if, after all, the claim turned out to be the unfounded accusations of a young boy's active imagination? But she felt she had to pursue legal action regardless of any slight degree of doubt she might have.

The disclosure that your child has been sexually molested is a shock. It produces grief similar to what one feels after a divorce or the death of a loved one. The recovery process takes time and requires the help of supportive professionals outside of your family.

Unfortunately, the most common initial reaction to learning about the abuse is to deny the need for outside help, feeling the situation is something that can be handled within the family unit. This is the time when family members often want to "circle the wagons" and isolate themselves from the outside, and even, unknowingly, from each other. *Resist this temptation.* Your survival instincts may not want you to do anything except express your sadness to your child and promise protection so that it will not happen again. You may get all kinds of pressures from family members and friends to limit your responses to only those actions. *Don't.* Outside help is needed because you, your child, and other family members may never fully recover unless you all have the opportunity to discuss what happened and how it has affected you with a qualified professional.

It is vitally important to report the offense, and many states have laws requiring such a report. It is estimated that only 5 percent to 10 percent of abusers are prosecuted. The reality is often that repeat sexual molesters have never been rehabilitated because no one ever took the action of reporting their previous abuses. Only if molestations are reported can authorities require that the abuser receive rehabilitative treatment—in the community or in the confinement of a correctional facility. Even if the molester is not legally an adult, it is still important for that child's actions to be reported.

Most experts now agree the most effective processing of an abuse case uses a team approach. Often this team involves:

the police

a child protective service social worker

an examining doctor

a legal representative of the state, such as a prosecuting attorney and, frequently,

a therapist

The description of the process that follows may not be exactly what you experience, but parts of it will apply to your case. Don't let the list or the process overwhelm or discourage you. In the long run, knowing what to expect will make it easier for you and your family to cope with the frustrations and strong feelings that can follow the reporting of an abuse. Don't let the necessary steps in the legal process discourage you from following through after you make the report.

Every community processes the investigation of a child's sexual abuse in a different way. Below are the steps that often follow, beginning with when authorities record the information from the report of an alleged molestation:

1. A report is made, usually by phone, to a local law enforcement office.

2. If the police or sheriff's department has the availability of a child protective service they call the service in to act as consultants to the law officers, or may ask the service to take the lead in processing the case. If available, this type of service usually offers unique facilities or skills that enhance the effectiveness of the law enforcement agency's processing of the investigation. The law agency might contact the protective service, or might ask the caller making the report to phone the intake department of that service.

Law enforcement will particularly wish to include the child protective service agency in the investigative process if the report indicates that the offender was a relative (and that is usually expanded to include extended family members and parents' boyfriends or girlfriends); a caretaker (someone to whom the parents entrusted the care of their child); or if information indicates that the parent(s) of the child will continue to place the child in a situation or place where the abuse could occur again.

3. In most states it is required that within a given number of hours an intake worker for the protective service or a police officer must talk with the child. This first meeting is to check out the details of the report and determine if there is cause to believe a molestation has taken place. The meeting is often brief and in a neutral setting, such as at school. Or parents may wish to bring their child to the agency's office instead. Workers can also visit the child's home, if the molester does not live there.

4. If there are indications that the child has been molested, the police officer and/or protective service worker will arrange a time with the child's parent(s) or primary caretaker to interview the child in a more formal manner. An arrangement may be made for a medical examination of the child to determine the presence of physical trauma and/or the child's general medical wellbeing, following the formal interview. In many cases it is recommended that the medical examination follow as soon after the formal interview as possible, to shorten the child's period of anxiety before the examination.

The formal interview may take place at the law enforcement agency, the offices of the child protective agency, or at the offices of an assisting consultative agency with which the legal jurisdiction specifically contracts to process sexual abuse cases (such as a Child Protection Team).

The interview may be videotaped to preserve the child's initial statement; this is becoming fairly common. (As a parent, your involvement is explained more completely in chapter 6, and Reality Check Number 8 will help you understand what behavior you can reasonably expect from your child during the interview(s).)

The child's safety should remain a primary concern. Following the formal interview, if the offender is living in the home:

- The offender will be asked to leave the home.
- If the offender refuses to leave, the nonoffending parent or guardian will be asked to leave the home with the child.
- If neither of these arrangements is possible, or the nonoffending parent is unable to protect the child, the child will be temporarily placed in what is felt to be a safe environment.

By law, there must be a hearing soon after any out-of-home placement in which the agency must justify to the court why this was done, and a determination made of the child's most appropriate residence.

5. After the interview (and examination, if required), the police officer and other agency personnel involved will decide if the information obtained justifies referral to the prosecuting attorney for a decision on bringing a criminal action against the alleged molester. (All of the references to "court" pertain to criminal court.)

If you are asked not to go to the newspapers with your story, or not to talk with other alleged victims' parents for now, there is usually a good reason. Cooperate.

6. A determination will be made by the prosecuting attorney (or equivalent state criminal justice official) whether to file criminal charges against the alleged molester. This decision is based on many factors, the strongest being the believability of the child's claims.

7. If the state decides to file charges, a warrant is sworn out for the arrest of the offender.

8. If there is no problem in locating the person, he or she is arrested.

If the abuser denies everything when approached by the arresting officer, after being read his or her rights, the opportunity to take a lie detector test may be offered. Most people decline, especially if represented by a lawyer. Lie detector results are not admissible in court, but the offender's failure to "pass" one may strengthen the prosecution's belief in the child's allegations.

The molester's denial is understandable. Think of all that person stands to lose if the victim's story is believed. Rejection by immediate and extended family is very likely. Professional standing and employment are in jeopardy. If found guilty of criminal sexual conduct, probation or prison is assured.

Besides these practical consequences of admitting guilt, there are psychological ones. Many abusers are so ashamed of their behavior they cannot admit it. For some, their shame forces them to continue to deny, even when there is overwhelming evidence of their guilt. Many abusers have character disorders that allow them to lie, convincingly and persistently, for months or years, in an attempt to convince others of their innocence. They may call upon their family and friends to provide character references and support. These may be given sincerely by people who truly believe the molester is innocent.

9. Within a period mandated by law, often twenty-four hours, the person must be brought before a judge or magistrate.

10. The judge reviews the booking report prepared by the arresting officer to determine whether there is probable cause to support the arrest. If probable cause is found, the judge sets the bond (which, when paid, allows the defendant to be released until trial) or holds the defendant over without bond (in which case he or she will be jailed).

11. At this first appearance, the defendant is given an arraignment date for the next court appearance. This may be a few days to several weeks away, depending on the court docket, or schedule, in the area.

12. Before the arraignment hearing, however, an offender who has retained a lawyer may consent to a prefiling agreement in which the defense and state attorney negotiate the plea and recommend penalty. The offender may agree to plead "no contest" (an admission that the charges are not

denied) in exchange for the state's recommendation to the court that he or she be placed on probation and court-ordered into an offenders' community treatment program (if there is one operating in the area).

13. If this happens, at the arraignment hearing the judge will hear the plea and listen to the prefiling agreement recommendations. A sentencing date will be set.

If agreement is reached between the judge and the attorneys, there will be no trial and the child will not have to testify. Sentencing completes the legal action on the case.

14. An arraignment hearing occurs regardless of whether there is a prefiling agreement. At the arraignment the offender will appear before a judge to hear the charges and plead guilty or innocent. If the offender has an attorney, they may waive the reading of the information and plead not guilty. Traditionally, defense attorneys have their clients plead not guilty, sometimes hoping to bargain on the charges later as the legal process proceeds.

If the defendant has not already engaged a defense attorney, he or she will be advised to do so. If, for some reason, the offender cannot, a lawyer will be appointed to represent him or her.

15. If no prefiling agreement has been reached, the trial date is set at the arraignment. How far in the future the trial will be is determined by the court docket (schedule) and also the constitutional guarantee of the right to a "speedy trial."

16. After the arraignment, the defendant's attorney will file a demand for discovery. This requires that all of the state's evidence against the offender must be made available to his or her lawyer: names of witnesses, copies of witnesses' statements, a taped or written copy of the interview with the child, etc.

17. Also after the arraignment, the attorney for the defendant may contact the prosecuting attorney and say something such as, "My client knows he (or she) messed up, and

is already in counseling." Sometimes the prosecuting attorney will contact the family to determine if they would like to see the case resolved quickly, without a trial. The legal right to make the final decision on whether the case goes to trial remains with the state, however.

If an agreement is worked out that does not involve a trial, the agreement is presented to the judge for approval. The family of the molested child might have had an opportunity to approve or disapprove the agreement, depending on the policy of the prosecuting attorney in that jurisdiction. If not, the family may be brought in at the time of the plea so the judge can hear their feelings about the agreement.

The agreement might include just a period of probation, and you and your family should be prepared for this possible disappointment.

18. Shortly before the trial date, a docket sounding (a conference between the judge, defense attorney, and prosecuting attorney) occurs to let the attorneys announce whether they are ready for trial. If not, they must give the reasons.

Frequently, the trial date is extended (continued) to allow both sides additional time for preparation.

19. If the case is continued, a new trial date is set. If the delay is caused by the defense, they may waive (give up) the defendant's right to a speedy trial.

(Further discussion in chapter 7 explains why the legal process often takes so long. Chapter 13 gives suggestions for preparing your child—and yourself—for a court appearance.)

20. If the case goes to trial, the judge may or may not appoint a guardian ad litem (a trained volunteer who works to protect the best interest of the child throughout the legal proceedings) for the child, with the parents' knowledge, through the juvenile court system. A guardian ad litem works with the child protection worker and prosecuting attorney to

monitor the court process and provide continued protection of the child and support to the family.

Often the case does not come to trial before six months after the charges have been filed against the offender.

21. If the alleged offender is found guilty, a sentencing date will be set. If the alleged offender is found not guilty, the case will be closed.

The description you just read covered criminal court actions, in which the state brings charges against the molester. There are other courts in which the family of a molested child could be involved.

Probate/juvenile courts rule on issues dealing with protecting the child. Protective service agencies, also responsible for the child's welfare, can gain court-approved temporary protective custody of the child and determine where he or she should live until other issues are decided.

Family court may become involved in cases in which the alleged molestation is interwoven with divorce or disputed custody, or in which visitation issues have arisen. Chapter 14 discusses these situations.

Civil court is a personal injury court in which lawsuits can be filed by individuals against perpetrators. Lawyers can be hired to advocate here for children if agencies fail to follow through, or if they feel the child is not properly protected. It is also where the family might sue for reimbursement of therapy expenses for their child and family and for other damages.

Though it is unlikely, a family could be involved in all four courts at the same time.

The investigative and legal processes take time—probably more than you think they should. It's a difficult time. The following chapters will help you understand why it takes so long, who the people are who will become involved with you in the process, and how to help your family cope emotionally during and after this period.

Janet and Bill were protecting their child when they phoned the police. Their action helped protect other children from possible molestation by the offender as well.

You have taken a very courageous and necessary step when you notify the authorities of the sexual molestation of your child.

3

Believing Your Child's Reality

WHEN children realize that something sexual has happened to them that makes them feel uncomfortable, it creates very confusing feelings. Until they share what has happened to them, children carry the burden of their abuse. (Some of the ways in which your child's behavior may indicate this burden are detailed in chapter 4.)

No matter *how* you hear about the molestation, your reaction to the information is very important in determining how your family will eventually heal. What your child needs most at this time is for you to take the burden from him or her. You need to provide assurance that what happened was completely the fault of the molester. And you must demonstrate to your child, by words and actions, that you will protect her or him from further abuse. Your child also needs to hear you say that you are aware that sharing the information took a great deal of courage.

Overreactions and comments such as "You'll never be the same!" or "That awful person has ruined you!" will only reinforce your child's feeling, as often related by formerly abused children, of being "damaged goods." When children hear well-meaning adults threaten to physically harm the molester, for instance, it only strengthens children's fears that the molester will seek them out and harm them, too. Although feeling helpless is a common reaction, this feeling should not be expressed in front of the child. Your child needs a calm protector who does not frighten him or her with hysterical rantings or overwhelming depression.

Also, children do not need to hear that their parents find it very difficult to believe their truth. Long interrogations will create great stress for your child. It can be very harmful if you use such phrases as "I just think this is unbelievable!" or "This can't be true." Children do not need to have anyone demanding to know why they did not tell someone sooner, either. This puts them in the position of feeling accused and guilty at a time when they so desperately need to feel believed and loved.

Research indicates that many of the children who report being sexually abused actually *minimize* the amount and type of the abuse. Exaggeration is very rare. It is felt that only two or three children per thousand make up events of sexual molestation or exaggerate what happened to them.

Reality Check Number 2:
What Are Some Helpful Phrases To Use with Your Child When First Told of the Molestation?

✔ "I know it took a lot of courage for you to tell what happened to you. What happened is not your fault. We're going to talk to someone about what you told us so that person will never hurt you or other children again."

✔ "We know how scary it must have been for you to tell what happened to you. We're going to talk to someone who can help us stop (the molester) from touching you or talking to you in a way that makes you feel uncomfortable again."

✔ "What a brave thing you did to tell us about what happened! That person knew what he (or she) was doing was wrong, and it wasn't your fault that he (or she) made you do things that made you feel uncomfortable. We'll see that no one does that to you again."

✔ "You were very smart to tell us what happened to you. Now we can help you and keep it from happening again. We know it isn't easy to talk about, but there are other people who need to know so that we can stop the molester from doing that again—to anyone."

It is important for your child to feel, right from the start, that the various agency representatives and investigative team members who will be involved are there to help. If you become frustrated or discouraged with the lengthy legal procedure, try not to telegraph these feelings to your child. Be as reassuring as possible to your child throughout the entire process. Be sure he or she knows that talking to other people about what happened and testifying in court (if it becomes necessary) are in no way "punishment" for what happened.

Reality Check Number 3:
What Is Sexual Molestation?

Most states (and it is incredible not to be able to say *all* states) have a legal definition for the molestation of a child. The definition is usually similar to:

✔ Sexual abuse is when any person, adult or child, forces, coerces, or threatens a child to have any form of sexual contact or to engage in any type of sexual activity at his or her direction. Keep in mind that while a child might be forced to cooperate, he or she is (by legal definition) not capable of giving consent.

✔ Involving children in inappropriate touching (clothed or unclothed), penetration using an object, forcing sexual activity between children, or asking the child to view or read or to participate in the production of pornographic materials is also molestation. *Asking* a child to have anal or oral sex (even if the act does not take place) is molestation, as is any form of bestiality (sexual activities with animals). Even when offenders insist they were gentle and did not physically hurt a child, these acts are molestation.

✔ A person commits the offense of child molestation when he or she does any immoral or indecent act to or in the presence of or with any child with the intent to arouse or satisfy the sexual desires of either the child or the person.

Obviously, it is not true that sexual molestation must involve sexual intercourse. The definition used by the National Center for Missing and Exploited Children for a child molester reads, "a significantly older individual who engages in any type of sexual activity with individuals legally defined as children." Some states define "children" as anyone under the age of nineteen, although in most states eighteen is the top age. In this definition "significantly younger" are key words. Some molesters are children, but their victims are *significantly younger* children. The ages of both people involved determine how significant the years between their ages are. Yet sexual activity between children becomes molestation when one child uses coercion to get the other child to comply with his or her demands. Young molesters should be reported to social service agencies so they can receive treatment and help.

Janet and Bill were unaware of the different types of molesters. (See chapter 1.) Their images of a molester were based on stereotypical movies and printed horror stories. It was certainly difficult to believe that the quiet, soft-spoken, sixty-five-year-old Mr. Webster fit the profile of a molester they imagined. They had always encouraged Scott to use his imagination. It would have been easy to tell Scott that he must have misunderstood what Mr. Webster had said or done.

Assessing a child's believability can be very confusing for parents. Young children (ages two to five) often *do* make up stories. These stories are frequently based on fairy tales or an imagined person, or are created because of a fear of being punished. Often children's stories are unconscious tries at comparing their realities with that of their parents, to determine if something they believe is true or not true.

It is important to allow children to be comfortable about divulging their "truths" to you as they are growing up. A child's "truth" is that child's interpretation of his or her world or what is happening in it. At four years old, one of Sara's truths was that she should be able to stay up late and watch television with her older sister on school nights. And she proclaimed it loudly. Her parents calmly explained to her that they understood that she really felt she should be able to do this. But until she was older, they reasoned, and required less sleep to stay awake in preschool the next day, she would have to go to bed early. Sara had a chance to state—and modify—what was "true" in her life. At least for now. She knew, too, she could test any of *her* future truths against the truths of her "all-knowing parents," and she would receive a loving response.

Sexual molestation is overwhelming to children because they grow up believing that adults are trustworthy and honest. After relying on adults to meet their survival needs since birth, children tend to believe what adults tell them is true rather than to rely on their own feelings. This works against them in two ways. If the molester tells them that what is being done is OK, they may doubt their own feelings that it is not. If parents' initial reaction when they hear the child's molestation

report is "This can't be true! He would never do something like
that!", the child may wonder if his or her own feelings are
mistaken.

Children almost never divulge an abuse "to create problems."
They more often fear they will make the person they tell
angry. *It is extremely difficult for children to report an abuse.*
Usually the molester—an adult authority figure—has told
them whatever happened is "all right" or has threatened them.
Children also feel embarrassed and ashamed. Because children
are naturally self-centered, they usually feel responsible for
what happens to them. They may feel that what has happened
proves they are "bad."

They are sometimes further confused by their own bodies.
Many molestations involve fondling or oral sex. Though it can
be terrifying to a child, their body may respond in the same
way it would to acceptable touching or cuddling and give them
a message of pleasure at the same time their brain tells them
that this is not right. All of this adds to the child's confusion.

Traditionally, children are taught to please adults. They can
also be intimidated simply by the much larger size of an adult,
with or without verbal threats.

Sixteen-year-old Tracy's molester (a stepfather who had
molested her since she was twelve) told her if she told anyone
she would be sent away to jail, and that her mother would die
if she found out what Tracy had done. Many teenagers are
surprisingly naive, though they are so often thought of as
sexually sophisticated. Raised in an isolated area, she had no
way to check the reality of what her stepfather told her.

A five-year-old boy was told he wouldn't get any more toys
from the molester (a family friend who regularly gave him
presents) if he told their "special secret." The boy finally told
when the man went away on an extended trip.

One molester threatened to kill a small girl's pet rabbits if
she told anyone. Jennifer became obsessed with having the
rabbits near her so she could protect them. When her mother
complained about the smell from the rabbit cage in her room,

Jennifer became alarmed and asked her mother if she was going to kill the rabbits. When her mother expressed surprise that she would even think that, Jennifer said the babysitter had told her she would kill the rabbits. Further questioning lead Jennifer to explain that the threat was connected to her not telling anyone about what the sitter had been doing to her.

It is not uncommon for molesters to tell children they will harm them or a loved one if they tell what's happening.

Mr. Webster made his molestations a part of the camping experience and bribed the boys with special awards and promises of trips. Because he was an authority figure and someone who first established a pleasant, nonsexual relationship with the boys, it was hard for them to question what he said. So when Mr. Webster told the boys that taking their clothes off was a part of camping, they didn't feel confident about their feeling that this was not right.

Webster was following the progressive seduction process often used by molesters who have frequent access to the same victims. This confuses children even more. A caring, affectionate adult who gradually introduces behaviors and requests the child finds uncomfortable can make the child question his or her own reasoning. Why would someone so kind and loving ask them to do something that was not OK?

Reality Check Number 4:
What Is the Usual Progression of Sexual Abuse?

There is a fairly predictable sequence of child sexual abuse. It is usually a relentless progression of sexual acts, from less to more intimate interactions, forced on a child by an overpowering adult. This overpowering can result simply from the fact that the adult *is* an adult, and does not necessarily indicate the use of threats, force, or other strong-arm tactics. Seldom is there any type of penetration in the first encounter. (Molestation accounts for 80 percent of sexual abuse, and child rape the other 20 percent.)

While many cases of abuse do *not* follow the progression all the way to penetration, the most typical sexual abuse progression is as follows:

✔ The perpetrator exposes himself or herself to the child, or views the child's body. The exposure can be done subtly (wearing loose-fitting clothing so that the genital area is exposed) or very obviously. Watching can take the form of the molester seeing a child undress or bathe or asking the child to remove clothing.

✔ The perpetrator usually touches his or her own body first, before touching the child. Because of this masturbation, there may be genital secretion on the hand touching the child.

✔ The perpetrator engages in touching, fondling, petting, stroking, or rubbing of the external genitals of the child, and has the child touch him or her.

✔ Usually the perpetrator has the child lick or suck his or her genitals, then has oral contact with the child's genitals.

✔ A male abuser often has dry intercourse—rubbing his penis on the child's body, between legs or buttocks or in the vaginal area, without penetration.

✔ With female victims, vulva-vaginal penetration begins with separation of the vulva, hymen, and vaginal area with a finger or lips and tongue before penetration of the vagina occurs with the penis or other objects.

✔ With male victims, the perpetrator may insert a finger, his penis, or an object in the child's anus.

Children seldom lie about being molested. They feel they have much more to lose than to gain when they reveal what has happened to them. When overpowered by a person of the same sex, children often fear it means they are homosexual, or that they'll be labeled as such if others become aware of it. Seldom, if ever, do children make up stories about their own sexuality. Most children do not have the knowledge to make up detailed "stories" of imaginary molestations. They may first report a molestation when abuse-prevention information or experiences in day care or school make them aware that what has happened to them is not normal.

Reality Check Number 5:
What Lifelong Problems Can Develop When Children Are Not Believed?

If children do not feel they can divulge the sexual molestation, or you do not believe them, they have no place to "take their truth." Without treatment, they grow up with lifelong problems.

✔ They don't trust themselves or their perceptions. A belief in one's self and feeling good about one's self are necessary for good self-esteem. Adults who were molested as children report feeling unlovable and lacking self-confidence because of the unresolved guilt and shame.

Elizabeth, now thirty-five, was told by her father at the age of fifteen—after he had molested her for ten years, that he would never molest her again, but no one would ever want her. He kept his word, but she grew up feeling unwanted and consequently sabotaged every intimate relationship until she found a therapist who understood that her sexual abuse was the cause of her low self-esteem and self-defeating behavior.

✔   They don't trust others. The first people a child trusts are adults. Adults who hurt children by violating their bodies and their minds (through confusion and/or threats) betray that trust.

Elizabeth's distrust of others made her feel people only wanted to be her friends to exploit and use her. She talked herself into being a "forever-victim." Her lack of self-esteem made her want to please people, but at the same time, she told herself that others were only out for what she could do for them and wanted to offer her nothing in return.

Jeff, too, never allowed anyone to get close to him. He had been molested by his much-admired piano teacher from ages six to nine, and learned then to detach the emotional part of himself during the physical sexual act. As an adult, he leads a life of "one night stands," and has experienced three failed marriages. Because of his childhood molestation, he fears emotional intimacy, and has conditioned himself to become detached or self-protective when he becomes involved with another person.

Even children who experience molestation for a shorter period of time and by someone less familiar to them can feel a lack of self-esteem and trust when adults do not acknowledge the molestation and provide for treatment.

Behaviors that result from not working through a sexual molestation can range from mild depression to having multiple personalities. As adults, molested people may experience flashbacks, sleep disturbances, and symptoms of anxiety or panic. Parents who do not attend to a child's sexual molestation are minimizing the child's reality and, without realizing it, being emotionally negligent to that child.

If families hush up the situation and do not allow their child's truth to be spoken and discussed, they are creating great anger and depression in that child that will become apparent in later years. This can lead to estrangement between the child and other family members. Families who do not accept and deal with their child's hurt are leaving themselves open to the child's expressing that hurt through running away from home, abusing alcohol or drugs, becoming promiscuous, marrying early, underachieving educationally and socially, acting out in violence and anger, or becoming a molester.

Children will try to suppress the pain that happens when they are hurt so badly and not believed. Not all children exhibiting the behaviors just described have been sexually molested. Yet it is common to find that children in residential treatment centers for disturbed children and in drug and alcohol rehabilitation centers are molestation victims.

Current reports indicate fictitious reports are uncommon. Those few that do occur are most often in disputed child custody cases (in which the child was coached by an adult) and in cases where older children who were previously abused falsely report that it is still happening.

It is important, however, not to jump to conclusions when your child says something that is unclear. From the first indication that there has been an abuse, don't assume that you know exactly what your child is "trying to say." If you state your assumptions as facts, you will confuse the situation and your child. Children often do not feel comfortable about correcting adults when they hear them describing things that didn't happen. Because adults are authority figures, children may begin believing that what a trusted adult is sincerely saying *is* true. Children may have been too embarrassed or scared to have told you *all* of the truth the first time. Once you've repeated their original story—or your interpretation of it—they may not feel comfortable telling the real version.

A classic example of a misunderstanding involves a mother whose three-year-old daughter told her, "When Daddy gets in the tub with me, we play games. Daddy has this long thing and we squeeze it and stuff comes out." The mother felt sick. She was ready to call the authorities. Fortunately, she asked Debbi to tell her once more what was happening. Debbi took her mother to the bathroom and showed her a nearly empty tube of shampoo. She and her dad had held it under the surface, let it fill with water, and then squirted each other—playfully and innocently.

Another mother was appalled when Stacey, her seven-year-old daughter, said, "Uncle Joe shows me his thing all the time in the bathroom." It was revealed that the uncle sometimes came into the bathroom to urinate while Stacey and his daughter were taking a bath in their one-bathroom house. Not appropriate behavior. Even poor judgment. But, in this case, it was done innocently and without any sexual intent.

When your child says something that could indicate sexual abuse, ask calm questions. Don't put words in your child's mouth. Don't sound as though you're accusing your child of doing anything wrong or as though you don't believe what is being said. Let your behavior indicate that you just don't fully understand and are interested in knowing more. Young children may not have the vocabulary to give much detail. Before you panic, be sure you understand what is really happening.

It may be better to call your area's child protection agency. Do this where your child won't hear any adult terminology you may use to describe what you think he or she said. Tell the agency you don't know exactly what your child is trying to say, and see if they can have a professional conduct an interview with your child to find out if there is a problem.

Again, while there may be some confusion about what happened, it is extremely unlikely that your child is making the whole thing up. Children have a difficult time tattling on adults or older children, and they have very little innate knowledge about sexual acts. When your child tells you what has happened, he or she risks many things: being called a liar, making you angry, losing the kind attention of the person who did the molesting (who may be someone very loved), and estrangement from other family members. The child may also fear being punished.

When children report molestation, it is because they realize they are in a situation they can no longer handle alone. People—even parents—sometimes withdraw emotionally from a molested child out of guilt or embarrassment. If your response is not supportive, your child will feel deserted and once again alone at a time when your support is vitally needed. Be there for your child, right from the time you first learn of the molestation. Sexual abuse is a burden your child should not have to carry alone.

4

Normal Sexual Development and Behaviors Indicating Possible Sexual Abuse

POSSIBLY you are wondering if something has happened (or is happening) to your child, but nothing has been said and you don't know if your suspicion has any foundation. It is important to be aware of your child's emotional and physical behaviors if you even *suspect* that he or she has been molested. If it is later confirmed, your observations can assist the professionals in their investigation, and can assist you in helping your child through the recovery period. The information given below can help you be more aware of your child's behaviors, and to recognize problems.

Before indicators of possible problems are discussed, sexual development that is considered "normal," by age, is detailed here as a Reality Check for you. These norms are not "rules." They are still being developed, and are subject to interpretation by those applying them—as are the indicators of possible abuse.

Reality Check Number 6:
What Is Normal Sexual Development by Age?

✔   Researchers have found that normal sexual development in humans begins while the fetus is still in the uterus. Ultrasound studies of male fetuses show reflex erections weeks before birth. It is believed that female fetuses have corresponding clitoral arousal and spontaneous vaginal lubrication as well.

✔   Soon after birth, infant penis and clitoral erections during nursing are normal. The warmth expressed through nursing is experienced as pleasurable by the babies, and arousal is a reflex reaction. Infants are unaware of these reflexes. As with many sexual behaviors in children, it is how parents react that may have the greatest affect on children.

✔   As the infants' motor systems develop, children will begin exploring their genitals and will receive pleasure from touching themselves. Orgasms have been observed in children under the age of one.

✔   By the age of two, most children can speak and walk and have a sense of being a boy or girl. They know this because they can see the difference in body parts. They express natural curiosity. It is sometimes a few more years before children learn to separate sexual behaviors between those publicly acceptable and those that should be private.

✔   From ages two to five, children are interested in their own genitals and those of others. They want to compare and explore genital areas through imitative games such as "doctor and nurse" and "mommy and daddy." Masters and Johnson's studies indicate that during these play activities they will look, touch, and sometimes attempt to insert objects into body openings. Children living in crowded housing often see adult sexual intercourse, and may mimic this behavior. They ask questions about birth and how babies are born. They believe that storks *do* bring babies, if that is what they're told, because they accept what parents tell them very literally.

They find the words for body parts very humorous and may develop a "bathroom sense of humor." Words such as butt, weiner, boobs, pee, toilet, and so on are hilarious to them.

✔ By the age of five, most children enter kindergarten and participate in more structured activities. They often develop more physical modesty, but the verbal jokes continue—even though they are not fully understood.

✔ At six and seven, children have a clearer understanding of the physical differences between the sexes and their sense of modesty becomes stronger. Natural curiosity is expressed through game playing again, with the same or opposite sex. Their purpose is just to seek knowledge. Sex play between two males or two females is in no way an indication of homosexual preference.

Children obtain pleasure from these activities and, when they represent mutual curiosity, this is normal. It is when one child becomes coercive (using threats or force) and is not acting out of curiosity that the activity becomes abusive. This most often occurs when there is a significant age difference, but if coercion is involved, even a child of the same age can be a molester.

✔ By eight and nine, children are aware of what is considered "sexy" by their society. Television shows, movies, and the behaviors of older people indicate to them which public—and private—behaviors between males and females have sexual overtones.

Experimentation goes underground as children become older and more aware of social rules. Formal games diminish, but children are still interested in exploration as it relates to stimulation. Mutual masturbation, especially among boys, is not uncommon. Because the opposite sex appears so scary at this time, they experiment with friends of the same sex because it is not as intimidating.

✔ As early as age nine or ten, some girls begin having menstrual periods. Boys may be having nocturnal emissions ("wet dreams"). Children are confused by the feelings that accompany these developments. They are confused about their own sexuality, about how their feelings relate to what they think are their parents' rules on sexual matters, and about the different emotions they are experiencing toward the same or opposite sex.

✔ Children may be surprisingly sexually naive, even though they are exposed to all the media emphasis on sexuality. Many times children are misinformed by other kids about pregnancy, venereal disease, or childbirth. Unless they get correct information, they may carry these myths into adulthood.

Parents of abused children from ages eleven to sixteen often incorrectly assume that their child knows what behaviors are inappropriate. They are amazed to find out he or she does not.

✔ During adolescence (when secondary sex characteristics develop: pubic hair and other body hair, breasts, testicle growth, etc.) children will experiment through dating, in groups or alone, in an attempt to establish their sexual identity. They will mimic the dress and behavior of people who appear to have established their independence—especially if it is an exciting, different expression of self. Through the years, Rudolph Valentino, Katharine Hepburn, Bette Davis, James Dean, Elvis Presley, The Beatles, Janis Joplin, Michael Jackson, and Madonna have been idols for teenagers seeking someone to imitate. This is because it is so hard in adolescence to decide on an identity that is original, in an attempt to establish separateness from parents.

With this understanding of what behaviors are considered part of normal sexual development, it is easier to be aware of behaviors that could indicate problems.

Reality Check Number 7:
What Behaviors and Conditions Might Indicate Your Child Has Been Sexually Abused?

Various lists noting physical and behavioral indicators of sexual abuse in children have been developed. It is generally agreed children might:

✔ Complain of pain while urinating or having bowel movements, indicating infection.

✔ Exhibit symptoms of genital infections, such as offensive genital odors, or symptoms indicating a sexually transmitted disease.

✔ Have symptoms indicating evidence of physical trauma (abrasions or lesions) to the genital area.

✔ Begin wetting the bed.

✔ Experience a loss of appetite or other eating problems, including gagging without a logical explanation.

✔ Show an unusual fear of being in a particular area of the house or some other place. If a young child is suddenly afraid of the bathtub or his or her bed, it can indicate that something disturbing happened there.

✔ Wake up during the night sweating, screaming, or shaking, or with nightmares.

✔ Masturbate excessively.

✔ Show unusually aggressive behavior toward family members, friends, pets, or toys.

✔ Engage in persistent sexual play with friends, toys, or pets.

✔ Have unexplained periods of panic, which might be flashbacks of abuse episodes.

✔ Regress to behaviors too young for the stage of development they have already achieved, such as thumb-sucking or talking very loudly.

✔ Initiate sophisticated sexual behavior (not developmentally appropriate for the child's age) toward other children or adults. For instance, professionals can pretty well determine that if a four-year-old child is trying to insert his penis into the rectum of a two-year-old boy or girl he has learned the behavior from someone. Caressing another child's genital area may be another indication for behavior not appropriate for the child's age. Wanting to stick his or her tongue into the mouth of another when kissing, or wanting an adult to rub the genital area is an indicator.

✔ Indicate a sudden reluctance to be alone with a familiar person.

✔ Engage in self-mutilation, such as sticking themselves with pins or cutting themselves with sharp objects.

✔ Withdraw abruptly from activity with a club or group that was formerly enjoyed.

✔ Ask an *unusual* amount of questions about human sexuality (particularly older—seven and up—children).

✔ Suddenly not perform as well in school.

✔ Show an unexplained change in personality traits. An outgoing, carefree child may become quiet and withdrawn.

✔ Develop an unexplained fear of males or females. Or a fear of men, for instance, with mustaches, or of men or women wearing a certain color or style of clothes.

✔ Make sudden requests for locks on the door and other safety precautions, and ask questions about protection.

✔ Express thoughts about death or suicide, or display suicidal actions.

✔ Develop an extreme fear of undressing in a physical education class or for a medical examination.

✔ Develop frequent unexplained health problems. The burden of carrying the molestation can stress the child into being unhealthy. Recurring stomachaches, headaches, and pains in muscles and bones that have no logical cause are possible indicators.

✔ Show symptoms indicating pregnancy.

✔ Not want to attend school, when this was not a problem before.

✔ Begin to abuse drugs or alcohol.

✔ Become unusually dependent on parents when they were previously more independent.

Any one of these behaviors by itself certainly does not confirm a sexual molestation. Key considerations are whether these behaviors are a dramatic change from a child's normal behavior, and how obsessive the new behaviors become to the child. The investigative teams will particularly want to explore any *changes* in behavior patterns you have noted. Children molested over a long period of time, however, may have a history of one or more of these behaviors, which will not stand out as a recent change.

Scott's withdrawal from the group he had previously enjoyed was a behavioral indicator that something was changing in his life, as were his questions about homosexuals. Had his parents not been open to pursuing Scott's comments, he might have taken much longer to reveal to them what had happened. If

Scott had grown up in a family that did not allow children to present their truths for reality checks by parents, he might never have felt that he could reveal the molestation.

You need to strike a balance between overreacting to unconfirmed indicators of abuse and ignoring them, without leaving unexplored the possibility that your child is being—and will continue to be—molested.

If you suspect a molestation, talk with your child in a nonthreatening, nonaccusing way. Indicate your concern, interest and support. Make it clear you don't think your child has done anything wrong. But give him or her the opening to say that someone is doing something that doesn't seem right. Say that even adults sometimes do things that aren't right, and that when that happens, other adults need to tell them they must stop.

If you and your child do become involved in an investigation, think back to when any of these behaviors might have started and let the investigators use the information in the ways they determine are best.

You can also use the list to mentally check your child's recovery. As these behaviors lessen or disappear, you can feel good about the progress your child is making toward recovery from the molestation.

5

The Professionals with Whom You Might Work

M ANY parents have had minimal contact with police officers and other investigative or child welfare professionals. This was true for Janet and Bill. Their concerns were how they could help Scott feel as comfortable as possible during the investigative procedures, understanding the roles of the different professionals with whom they would be working as the case proceeded, and helping investigators as much as possible.

The agencies and individuals in their community who were involved in the report of a sexual molestation were:

Paul Adams, a sergeant with the Criminal Investigation Department of the county sheriff's department;

Sally Johnson, the intake social worker for the state Human Services agency;

Barbara Turner, case coordinator with the state consulting Child Protection Team;

Jon Devlin, M.D., pediatrician/consultant working under contract with the Child Protection Team;

Brenda Hunter, Assistant State Attorney;

Michael Phelps, M.S.W., therapist, working under contract with the area's sexual abuse treatment program.

Scott would interact with at least these six strangers, and it could be an understandably confusing situation for him if he and his parents were unclear about the roles of each of these professionals. Although the professionals involved and their roles will vary greatly from area to area, the following provides an explanation that should help you in the investigative process you encounter.

Sgt. Adams was assigned to investigate the report phoned in by Janet. In their area, this was a function of the sheriff's department. In other locations, this might be handled by a city police officer. In many places, the same officers must handle cases ranging from burglaries to traffic violations—along with child abuse reports. They may have received no intensive training to prepare them for the specialized field of child molestation investigation. Fortunately, law enforcement agencies are becoming more aware of the need for special training in the investigation of sexual abuse allegations, including the interviewing techniques best suited to working with children. Increasingly they are sending their personnel for that training.

Sally Johnson is a child advocate representative of the state through her role as intake worker at the local office of the state's Human Services agency. Almost every community has some form of child protective service monitoring the physical, emotional, and sexual protection of children. Some communities call this service simply Children's Services. In others it is a division of the state or county child welfare system. Some children's service agencies are county agencies and others are operated by the state, depending on the governmental structure.

Intake workers at these agencies have the authority to assess the child's welfare and take legal action to provide continued protection to the child. This is done on a temporary basis, until a court order supporting their decision is obtained or denied. Sally will be involved because Mr. Webster was considered to be in a "caretaker" position. A person with the child welfare department is usually involved if the molester is either a custodial person or a relative.

As a representative of an agency hired to consult with both law enforcement and human service agencies, Barbara Turner of the Child Protection Team will assist Sally and Sgt. Adams by providing her agency's interviewing room for the formal interview and will schedule Scott for a medical examination. (In other areas, this agency might have been called by such names as Advocacy Team, Advocacy Center, Sexual Assault Team, or Children's Crisis Unit.) Barbara, highly skilled in interviewing children, may or may not be asked to lead the interviews with Scott. In her role of providing legal, psychological, and medical services for abused children, she will act as a liaison, if requested, between the state attorney's office, sheriff's department, and doctor. This agency has only the authority delegated to it by the other agencies for whom it works. Some Child Protection Teams have an attorney on retainer to provide legal advice as needed both in court and out. Barbara will also refer the family to a public or private therapist.

Dr. Devlin contracts with the Child Protection Team, through his private practice, to examine children for possible physical trauma that may be related to sexual abuse. Even children who are believed to have been just fondled are often examined. This can provide children with a source of information from a person they see as an expert. (One nine-year-old girl believed she was pregnant, not knowing it could not happen from fondling. She was reassured after hearing, *from a doctor*, that it was impossible, and that she had not been physically harmed.) In some communities, the county health department may be responsible for conducting the examination. In other areas, a doctor may be on-staff with the agency and limit his or her practice to examining children who have been sexually abused. On-call doctors in a hospital's emergency room provide this service in some areas.

Brenda Johnson, Assistant State Attorney, becomes involved in assessing the evidence from the above sources to see if prosecution of the case appears justified. (Depending on area, this person could be called a district attorney (D.A.), prosecutor, prosecuting attorney, county attorney, or other title. If there is a large staff, they may have attorneys specifically trained to work with these cases. Smaller staffs will require their personnel to handle a wide range of cases, without specific expertise.) Brenda will review the report and the videotape (if one is made) in preparing any criminal charges against the alleged offender. She will present and argue the case in court, if the case goes that far.

Michael Phelps, M.S.W. (Master of Social Work) is licensed in his state as a marriage and family therapist. He is also in private practice and does work under contract with the Child Protection Team. Michael received special training in the treatment of sexually abused children and their families. Some communities offer treatment through a local mental health center at no cost, or for a sliding-scale fee based on income. Other communities will simply recommend private practitioners who provide services at their usual fees. Michael will be helping Scott and his family members to resolve the family hurt caused by the abuse.

The services available to Scott and his family are nearly ideal, based on current findings in the areas of investigation and treatment of sexual abuse. In many areas parents may have contact only with a police officer. Some communities offer the services of a welfare agency worker who must be responsible for many other jobs. Many communities do not have the luxury of having a consultative agency such as a Child Protection Team. Even in some areas where the various agencies exist, they do not operate as a single team. Every community differs in its support sources and its approach to the investigation process.

You may have to accept the reality that specialized professional agency assistance is limited in your area. There may be no Child Protection Team and no Sexual Abuse Treatment Program. You may not have access to mental health professionals with expertise in sexual abuse counseling. This can be very frustrating, both for you and for the professionals you *will* deal with. They realize they can't possibly do everything for molested children and their families that they would like to do, simply because of too many demands on their time and too little specialized training.

This does not mean that *you* can't work, with whatever assistance *is* available to you, to keep the molestation and investigative process from affecting your family in the least traumatic way possible.

6

How to Help Investigators Work Effectively with Your Child

WHETHER you work with a team of professionals or just one, all investigators agree it is vitally important that parents do not question their child at length before the official interview takes place. Don't keep going over the facts of what happened with your child unless he or she brings it up, but don't pretend it didn't happen either. Children pick up on your conversations with others, in person or by phone, and also on how you feel about what happened. *Be careful.* Many cases cannot be prosecuted because of the sophisticated language a child picks up from intense conversations with parents or other adults regarding the incident(s). Even overhearing a phone call in which you use adult words (which your child later repeats— even though he or she really doesn't understand them) may invalidate your child's testimony.

Prosecutors are often bewildered by family reactions. In cases of the most awful abuse, some families are not at all supportive of their child. In other cases that involve only inadvertent touching over clothing, the family demands the electric chair. Be reasonable. But *think of your child's welfare first*, not yours or anyone else's.

Be careful to keep your responses to your child's information from appearing threatening or blameful. Your child may change the initially true story of what happened if you appear to disapprove. And your feelings are expressed as much by how you *act* as by what you *say*.

After you have reported the abuse, when you are called back by the investigator to make an appointment for the formal (possibly videotaped) interview, be sure to let the scheduling person know what times of day are best for your child—based on naps, mealtimes, school, etc. A tired or hungry child does not interview well. If your child has particular fears (of men, of women, of someone in uniform), tell the person calling. During this phone conversation, it is a good idea to ask how long the interview will take, who will be there, and if your child will be going for his or her medical examination right after the interview.

Before or after your child's interview, you will probably be asked to discuss the allegations of the abuse with the professionals. Separate from your child, you will be asked what you know about the report, what behavior changes you may have noticed, how your child is now behaving, and whether you feel the allegations are true. It is a good idea at this time to have a written list of any questions you've thought of to ask the investigators. Keep a notebook of your questions and the answers you are given. It is also a good idea to record the names and phone numbers of the professionals working with your child. Each time you have contact with one of them, find out what the next step in the process will be, and ask whom you can contact about the progress of the investigation.

Before the interview, it is helpful to your child to know how many strangers he or she will be meeting. In some communities only one person conducts the interview, or you may be able to request that this be the procedure. Whoever will be interviewing needs to explain to your child (in a way appropriate for his or her age) where they will be talking, how the interview will be conducted, and about how long it will take. To decrease anxiety about being videotaped, ask that your child be shown the camera in advance—if this is not automatically done. He or she should also be allowed to see any toys (possibly anatomically correct dolls) that will be used. The child should also understand that you will not leave the nearby waiting area during the interview.

Anatomically correct dolls often help children identify body parts, especially children ages two to five with limited ability to describe in words what happened to them. They also provide children with a way to show what happened when they are too embarrassed or afraid to say what was done. Very young children may have problems using the dolls because of difficulty in thinking of the dolls as themselves. They may be more comfortable using their own bodies or pointing to parts of the interviewer's body to explain the abuse. Anatomically correct drawings, used in the same way, usually work well with children six to eight years old.

Your state may have a limit on the number of times a child can be interviewed as a part of the investigative process. This can make things easier on your child and your family. It also forces the interviewing team to get organized before they begin. By limiting the number of times your child is interviewed, agencies may be more effective in getting the information they need and maintaining cooperation from your child. A single interview, when conducted properly and recorded on videotape or audiotape, offers the advantages of reducing the number of times your child has to tell his or her story, and preserves the statements for future review by agencies or the court.

Preserving the initial interview on videotape also lets the prosecuting attorney review the allegations against the abuser and get an idea of how effective your child may be as a witness. The legal validation of your child's sexual abuse may depend entirely on the investigative interview, so it is very important.

Understand that it may be difficult for the interviewer to get the needed information from your child for several reasons. Children who must repeatedly tell their stories of the abuse may think they are not being believed. As a result, they may begin to hold back information, may add made-up "facts," or may change to answers they feel the interviewers want to hear. Abused children have often been told repeatedly by the molester—usually a person representing authority to the children—"not to tell anyone." It can be very difficult for children to go against these instructions. Children often feel they are the guilty ones in the abuse. They may have known that what was happening was wrong, but they did not find the abuse painful or bad. This can be very confusing to them, and can make the molestation harder to talk about.

Reality Check Number 8:
What Are Realistic Expectations for Your Child's Behavior during an Investigative Interview?

Your child's age will be one determining factor in how cooperative he or she can be during the investigative interview(s).

✔ Obviously, children who have not yet learned to communicate with words make it difficult, at best, for investigators.

✔ Verbal communication usually becomes possible with children sometime between the ages of two and four.

✔ Children two to four often do not understand concepts well, even though their language skills may seem to indicate that they do.

✔ Preschoolers can usually concentrate on just one thought at a time.

✔ Very young children often tire of talking about what happened to them and become silent and withdrawn during the investigation interviews.

✔ Children have limited patience in answering repeated questions.

✔ Children may give different answers to the same questions, depending on how they are asked.

✔ Even though preschoolers spend much time in play centered around fantasy, they can usually distinguish fact from fantasy quite clearly.

✔ If an association can be made with something else, preschoolers can often recall isolated events quite vividly.

✔ Nearly all children are embarrassed, and they seldom have the "right" words to explain what happened. It's not that they *won't* express what happened; they *can't*.

✔ Young children tend to ramble when telling their stories, and will commonly include information you and the investigator do not feel has any connection with what happened.

✔ Four- to six-year-olds have concepts of distance, time, and space only as they can perceive it applying to them personally.

✔ Children usually see adults as all-knowing and, for that reason, feel that adults can tell when they are lying.

✔ Children ages six to eleven can understand the interview process and be more helpful.

✔ It's easy to *say*, "Let the child tell his or her own story," and insist that the investigator not ask "leading" questions (questions that tend to indicate the answer that is wanted or to supply some of the information needed to answer the question), because that can be considered as making a child's statements less valid. Yet young children, particularly, may almost *have* to be led by the questions they are asked to obtain any information about what happened.

One Child Protection Team worker stressed how important it is to assure children, especially young children, that their taped interview won't be on people's television sets. They may feel that, having been taped, it will now be on their television set at home and in other people's houses like the news. Sometimes it may help to tell young children that the television set in the interview area is a special one that their tape can be shown on, but that it will not be shown on anyone else's, anywhere.

It is often easier for children to tell something to someone they don't know than to someone they love. Children may be less embarrassed talking to investigative team members who are total strangers. These professionals usually try to make children feel they can express themselves freely. They let the child know they've talked to hundreds of other kids who've been through the same thing, that nothing the child says can shock them, and that any words the child may use they've heard many times before.

More than likely, you will *not* be allowed to be with your child during the interview. Parents sometimes, even without planning to, react to what their child says while being interviewed. Either with words—making corrections, additions or deletions to the child's story—or with facial expressions that indicate embarrassment, horror, or disgust. This can influence what the child says. Children aged two or three may need a parent or familiar person with them before they will feel safe enough to talk. If so, that person should sit close to the child, supportive but silent.

If your child has expressed concerns or questions, try to get the answers to those questions *before* the interview begins. You can ask the questions with your child present (if you feel this would be the most helpful in alleviating your child's anxiety), or you can ask them alone and report the answers back to your child.

It is desirable for the person(s) interviewing your child to be as patient and calm as possible. If your initial contact with them indicates that they are rushed, stressed, or too brisk, you have the right to request that the interview be postponed to another time.

After the interview, the investigators will probably want to speak with you alone again. This is your opportunity to ask for their recommendations of therapists who are trained specifically in the area of sexual abuse, if this assistance has not already been offered. You should arrange to begin immediate professional counseling for your family.

You will probably be curious as to whether the investigators feel confident that this case can be taken to court. Don't be discouraged if their answers appear to be vague. They will probably want to review and discuss your child's statements before they decide to present the case to the assistant state's attorney. If the investigators say they will "get back to you soon," ask them to be more specific. Approximately *when?* Before leaving the interview, write down everyone's name and phone number so you'll know whom to contact as you have questions in the future.

It is normal for your child to be anxious before and after the interview. Try to keep your responses to his or her feelings calm and reassuring. Investigators stress that behaviors such as crying or shouting in your child's presence will only increase his or her fears and worries.

After the interview and medical examination, your child may be unusually quiet or anxious. Allow your child to express his or her feelings as needed at this point. A stop for a hamburger, a quiet talk, having a story read aloud at home, or the chance to be alone may be helpful to your child. Continue to reassure your child that telling his or her truth was the right thing to do, and that you realize it took courage.

Be careful not to interrogate the child after the interview. A simple question such as, "Do you feel sad right now or do you feel glad?" is appropriate; one like, "Did the policeman tell you he was going to put that bad person in jail?" is not.

You may find your child appears relieved after being interviewed. If you have offered support from the beginning, the relief indicates that your child feels good that you have been protective, and that someone has listened to his or her truth. Be careful not to represent the interview as the end of the process your child must face. The reality is that your child may be asked to go through more interviews, give a deposition, or be a witness at the trial. Another possible outcome is that the process may be dropped entirely. If it is dropped, be prepared to deal with your child's possible disappointment—and your own.

One couple said they wished they had known they could have asked investigators questions about the progress of the case. Had they felt comfortable in doing so, they would not have felt the frustration they experienced when they heard nothing about the case for long periods of time.

Some parents have wished they had not let their child see how upset they were, because they realized afterward that it frightened their child. Comments from parents reflecting on the early stages of the legal process include:

• "I was so caught up in my own confusion and anger that I didn't realize how badly my child needed me for support. After the interview, I drilled my child about everything she had said. I wanted to make sure the molester was punished. I didn't realize I was making her feel personally responsible for seeing that he went to jail."

- "We wish we had stressed to our child that the investigators were friendly people who just wanted to help. And that the presence of a policeman didn't mean she had done anything wrong."

- "When I discovered my child had forgotten to tell the investigators about the babysitter telling her to keep the abuse a secret, I'm sorry I told her it would be all her fault if he was never punished. I realize now what an awful thing that was to do."

- "I felt my child's description of what happened wasn't clear, so I described to her what I thought she meant. When she was interviewed, she used my words. The case was dropped because they felt my child had been coached."

The investigative stage can be incredibly confusing. You may meet and have to work with several different strangers, none of whom can give you a clear answer at this time of what will finally happen. It is normal for you to feel frustrated and angry. Share these feelings with those you think will best understand: your spouse, your intake worker, your therapist. Be sure to keep your feelings in check around your child. Your child will understand your expression of a reasonable degree of concern, but be careful to express your deeper frustrations and emotions only to other adults.

Once you've gotten through the initial interviews, congratulate yourselves on completing the second step in your family's recovery.

Then take a deep breath, and prepare yourself for the painfully slow grinding of the wheels of justice that almost inevitably follows. The next chapter explains the delays you may encounter—and why—and offers helpful suggestions for how to cope constructively with the frustrations you may experience.

7

Why Does Everything
Take So Long?

IMMEDIATELY after you first become aware of your child's molestation, much of your life will seem to center around that concern. Once you report the molestation, you will become involved in investigative and legal processes and ways of seeking help for your child and your family. It is understandably a time of chaos and frustration. Although the usual responsibilities of your life go on, many more are *added*. It can put a severe strain on you and your family to have to cope with extra demands on your limited time, especially at a time when you are all so emotionally upset. It can become even more frustrating when the progress of the "official" aspects of the molestation—the investigation and the legal process—seem to move so slowly.

People often unconsciously expect things to happen as they do on television. On television the crime happens, the police solve the case, the person goes to trial and is sentenced, and the victim returns to a normal life—all in a speeded-up sequence that can be portrayed in half an hour, an hour, or two hours. Though parents may recognize on a conscious level that things don't happen this way, the apparent speed in these dramas can unconsciously affect expectations.

In real cases, steps proceed with frustrating slowness. Everything must be done in prescribed ways and in a certain sequence. Any delay in one of the steps along the way delays the entire process waiting to follow.

After Scott's initial interview, Bill and Janet heard nothing from the Child Protection Team worker for several days. When Janet phoned the prosecutor's office, she was told the investigators had not yet finished interviewing all of the children in Scott's camping club, and they would not proceed until that was completed.

Her next call, to the police department, was transferred from one person to another. She could not remember the name of the officer who had been at the interview. She was finally told only that they were working on the case to the fullest extent their time and staff allowed. She felt she had gotten a standard answer from someone who wasn't even familiar with the case. She and Bill felt very helpless in not being able to make the wheels of justice turn faster. Didn't anybody care what had happened to their son and the other boys?

When Bill came home from work the next day, he found Janet angrily typing a letter to the judge who had set bail for Mr. Webster. She demanded to know how he could let a man like that roam the streets and endanger other children.

It wasn't until their counseling sessions with Michael began that they finally let go of the need to feel they had to have complete control over the situation. With his help, they began concentrating on healing the family hurt. The legal aspects of the molestation were no longer their main focus and their frustration diminished.

The fact that things happen slowly doesn't necessarily mean that the professionals involved aren't doing their jobs or that they don't care. If everything were rushed, only chaos would result. Slowness can be an indication that the agencies involved are doing their jobs very carefully. If they don't gather all of the necessary facts and evidence *before* they request that charges be filed, for instance, the case may not be substantial enough to convince the prosecutor's office that charges are justified.

There is wide variation from state to state in the ways

prosecutors' offices handle cases. The attitude of the local office toward sexual molestation cases makes the difference. In some cases, they will review the evidence and suggest to the investigative team what additional statements (if available) would give them the material they feel is necessary to file charges and get a conviction. Other prosecutors leave it totally up to the investigators to gather and prepare the information in the case, then rule on whether it is sufficient to justify a warrant and trial only after it has been officially presented to them—with no second chance if they feel it is insufficient.

It can be a difficult decision for prosecutors to make. Their offices are usually *very* busy. If investigative agencies routinely refer cases to them in which there is no chance of obtaining a conviction, they waste valuable time that is needed on other cases. Yet if agencies take the wrong steps in the investigative process because they haven't had sufficient advice from the state's attorney, investigators can sometimes mess up the legal aspects of the case to the point of making a conviction impossible. In some communities an effective working relationship has been developed between investigators and prosecutors; in others, unfortunately, this is not yet true.

Once your child is considered to be in a safe environment, the investigation need not be as rushed. Allowing adequate time makes better coordination between the agencies involved possible. The interview(s) can be scheduled so that the investigative team can meet beforehand to determine the exact information they need in your child's case. The lack of a rushed feeling also lets the interviewer establish a better rapport with your child during the actual interview session.

The time between the awareness of what has happened and the arrest may actually be quite short. If it is determined there is probable cause to suspect the molester, a warrant for arrest can be obtained. If the person has not fled the area, it's simply a matter of serving the warrant and arresting the offender. Understandably, there can be delays when molesters deliberately make themselves difficult to find.

It's the period between the arrest and the final outcome of the case that can be so difficult for you and your family. Unfortunately, for many families everything else takes on less importance during this time than trying to see that the molester is "appropriately" dealt with by the legal system.

It can certainly be hard to understand why a neighbor who molested your child and was arrested in the morning can be back mowing his lawn and glaring at you in the afternoon. Yet it has to be accepted as an application of a constitutional protection guaranteed to all of us.

Our legal system allows people charged with most offenses to bail or bond themselves out of jail. You may feel the abuser should not have this right, but it is guaranteed by the law. Even those guilty people charged with abusing children have the same rights under the law that you would have if wrongly charged with that offense. Those rights must be protected to keep them available to the innocent, even if the guilty benefit from them in the meantime.

Other aspects of the legal proceedings and rulings also may be confusing to you. For instance, the particular sentence a child molester faces varies from state to state, and depends on such factors as the nature of the abuse and the abuser's prior criminal record. Many states have adopted sentencing guidelines in an attempt to standardize the sentences received by all individuals who commit a particular crime. Such guidelines provide a degree of certainty to the sentence faced by a defendant in a criminal case, but they also severely limit the judge's discretion in imposing what he or she feels is the appropriate punishment for a particular offender.

As difficult as it may be to accept, if you can realize that you have very little control over what happens to the molester—even if he or she is eventually convicted—you will be able to direct your energies to helping your child and your family cope with and recover from the molestation.

This does not mean that you should not cooperate in every way possible with the investigative team and other authorities.

It just means that you have to "let go" of feeling personally responsible for punishing the molester and decide that whatever the system and the state eventually do to that person is really beyond your control.

Answer the questions of the professionals and give them any information you feel will help. Also give them time. That doesn't mean that some people won't drag their feet unnecessarily. The system isn't perfect, but in the end it usually works. Let them do their job in the way they determine is best. Realize that the system doesn't move quickly and it doesn't work to everyone's satisfaction. It has inherent flaws. Because the abuse is affecting your life so greatly, it is easy to forget that other families are going through the same thing and there are usually not enough personnel or time to allow the agencies involved to handle cases promptly.

It's not unusual for a trial to be held a year after the time of arrest. Although it can be a difficult time, sometimes the delay can work to your advantage. It can be a time during which you and your child can put some psychological distance between you and what happened. The difficult part is having the legal issues remain unresolved all that time.

If you can keep your main focus on helping your child and your family during this time, the often slow legal process will present fewer frustrations for you. Resist the temptation to let frustration—and not more valid reasons—influence you to try to get the trial cancelled. Usually it *is* important for the molester to be officially charged with the crime and properly sentenced.

If you find yourself engulfed by feelings of frustration and confusion over the legal process, first try to redirect your thoughts and energies to your child's needs and your own. If you find you're so frustrated by legal delays that you can't concentrate on anything else, a little prodding, if you feel it's really necessary, might not be out of line. A phone call to the appropriate agency to inquire about the status of your case can be extremely helpful to you and your child. You will feel you have at least gotten *some* feedback, and that should lessen your anxiety. If you are tempted to go to the newspapers in an attempt to get action, but the authorities ask you not to, ask the reasons for their request and, if they are reasonable, do as they ask.

If any additional information comes up after the initial interviews or investigation and before the trial, let one of the professionals working on the case know about it immediately. Refer to your notes listing the names of the people working with you to decide whom to call.

Different jurisdictions give parents differing amounts of input into decisions about the case once it is in progress. Officially, a criminal case represents the state's actions against the accused, something taken totally out of the hands of the victim or victim's family. Yet in some places, the wishes of the family are taken into consideration as the case proceeds. *If* the decision is left up to you, and *if* you decide you will be satisfied with accepting a guilty plea and having the abuser receive a probationary term and mandatory participation in a treatment program rather than being jailed, let the authorities know this as soon as possible. This will allow you to spare your child the depositions, interviews, and other constant retellings of the story that may not be necessary if there is to be no trial.

Once you have decided to follow through and go to trial, it will involve depositions of your child and anyone else felt to be a key witness; possible testimony of your child in court (if videotaped testimony is not allowed or felt not to be as effective in your child's case); and all the legal procedures of any criminal trial. It's important to try to understand the process and to be patient. (See chapter 13 for a more detailed description of procedures you and your child may be involved in before and during a trial.) The process will not be fast and it will not always be pleasant. *If* the decision is left up to your family, only you can decide what is best.

In some jurisdictions, defense attorneys get all of the continuances (approved delays of the trial date) they request. This depends on the practices of the presiding judges. If judges feel that denying continuances will result in later appeals of guilty verdicts on the grounds that the defense did not have adequate time to prepare for trial, you can understand why they (even if reluctantly) often grant requested continuances.

A judge relates, "It's a heartbreaking thing for a judge to come into a trial where witnesses are subpoenaed and assembled and the jurors are available, but one or the other of the legal teams is not ready. Because we're dealing with lawyers and prosecutors who often have heavier case loads than they ought to have, we grant a continuance. We are left with little choice because there are serious rights and consequences involved. All of those people get called off, and they can't possibly understand why these things have to happen. Often it's a question of resources. If we had more prosecutors, more public defenders, more court-connected counselors and evaluators, more judges and more specialization of judges, we could change things. Inadequate staffing—because of lack of funds— is the base problem."

Defense attorneys often see delays as working to their advantage. They feel the longer a trial is delayed, the more tired the victim's family will become of the whole process. They sometimes think if it takes long enough they can even convince the family not to go through with it. In fact, they sometimes tell families that if they don't want to go through with depositions or repeated interviews they can just drop the case. If it is a criminal case, this is technically not true. A criminal case is filed by the state. It is *the state's* case, though the state will often take into consideration the feelings of the families of molested children, even more than it might the feelings of other victims of crime, in deciding whether to proceed to trial.

One assistant state attorney says, "If people are putting a lot of pressure on the family to drop the case, I remind them to tell people that the decision is the state's, not theirs. Some state attorneys even tell mothers (or other family members being heavily pressured to drop the case) to place a call to them *in the presence of the people applying pressure* and say 'I want the case dropped.' This can help get those people off their backs. Then they can call back later, when they're alone, to say how they *really* feel." Be careful that you do not mislead the prosecuting attorney you're working with by doing this *without* agreeing to this tactic in advance.

The passage of time nearly always works primarily to the advantage of the defense. Defense attorneys routinely request continuances. The defense will also often waive the speedy trial requirement. Once that happens, there is no clock running for anyone, and the overburdened system can really slow down. During that time, your emotions will probably become less vehement and memories of details will fade. This is what the defense is hoping for.

While it is understandably frustrating, the best thing for you to do is to remind yourself that there is almost nothing you can do to rush the system. Don't try to exert control over a system that you are pretty helpless to affect.

Your family will probably get emotionally "geared up" once the trial is scheduled. If the defense attorney can get the trial postponed, he or she knows your emotions will plummet. And you will have to live with knowing that you have to get yourself emotionally prepared for the court proceedings all over again. If this trial roller coaster of scheduled date / emotional preparation / postponement / frustration happens a couple of times, you can get very tired. And discouraged. And bitter.

During this time, devote your efforts to the part of the situation over which you *do* have control: helping your child and your family. If you feel you are doing something positive, the slowness of the legal process won't be quite as frustrating.

The date for the trial of Scott's molester was changed three times. It was Michael's counseling that made this difficult period more bearable for the Thompson family. Because they could see the progress they were making in how they related to one another, and they felt good about how Scott was getting back to his usual smiling self, waiting for the trial was pushed to the sidelines of their life. Try to let it be that way for you.

8

Steps to Healing: The Grief Process

However you heard about your child's molestation, your first feeling may have been that of disbelief, even verging on shock. The emotions you go through after learning about the molestation are very similar to the feelings of grief connected with a loved one's death or with the end of a special relationship. Other family members will experience varying degrees and stages of grief, also.

It is important for you to work through these stages so that you heal yourself, and assist your family members in healing, too. While each individual must work through the process in his or her own way, it is important to seek the help of a competent therapist to help guide the progress.

Detailed here is the grief process that most parents experience after learning their child has been molested. The stages of the process include shock, denial, anger, guilt and depression, bargaining, and—finally—acceptance.

Shock and Denial

Often parents, when presented with the information about their child's molestation, will listen carefully, ask fairly clear questions, and appear outwardly calm. Inside, they are attempting to substitute in their minds what they would *rather* have heard for what they were *actually* told.

When Scott reported that Mr. Webster had touched him inappropriately, Bill listened to what Scott had to say in a calm manner and responded to him appropriately. Yet in Bill's mind he was thinking what Scott said could very possibly have been in Scott's imagination because Bill had such a positive image of his own childhood camping leader. At the same time, he was picturing Mr. Webster at the last parents' meeting, and finding it difficult to connect Mr. Webster's gentle, almost meek, manner with his image of how a child molester "should" be. Bill's shock reaction came when he actually pictured Mr. Webster touching Scott in a sexual way.

Other parents tell how they reacted:

• "When I found that my father-in-law had fondled my daughter's breasts, I was dumbstruck. I had noticed that he singled out Jennifer for some reason, but I had no idea it was not just because she was especially sweet."

• "Jimmy, our babysitter, was great with the kids. He was athletic, clean-cut and appeared to be the 'All-American' sixteen-year-old. When my kids reported to us that Jimmy had molested them, I kept asking if they could have him confused with somebody else. I just couldn't believe it."

• "Jeremy seemed like such a harmless man. He was everyone's 'Good Neighbor Sam.' What a shock when we parents discovered he had molested our children. It was not only hard to believe, we didn't want to believe it."

Reality Check Number 9:
How Are the Feelings of Shock and Denial Sometimes Expressed in the Grief Process?

While you are feeling shock, you might find yourself:

✔ Calling several people, including your child's social service worker, to ask if he or she really thinks your child's story is true.

✔ Experiencing alternating feelings about your child's story: shock when you visualize what you've been told, and denial when you think about what a nice person the accused molester appears to be.

✔ Feeling strongly that you want to keep the information from family members and friends.

✔ Being tempted to question your child over and over about what he or she has reported. (Don't.)

✔ Needing to get all of the information you can find about sexual molestation and molesters.

✔ Wanting to take your child and leave the community.

✔ Having feelings that it's all a bad dream, and that when you wake up tomorrow you'll discover it never happened.

Anger

Bill and Janet discussed their shock and amazement that Mr. Webster could be hurting their son. As they spoke with each other and accepted that it had actually happened, they began to feel rage. Janet's rage was expressed by sobbing and Bill's by pounding the kitchen table. They felt betrayed. Their belief system about what was good for their son was badly shaken. They had been so sure that the camping experience would be a valuable one for Scott. Instead, it had turned into a nightmare for all of them. Janet and Bill wanted to see Mr. Webster in jail—forever.

Parents explain the anger they felt:

• "If my wife hadn't asked me for my gun, I'm afraid I may have shot my child's molester. I wanted to kill him. He took away my child's innocence."

• "I hoped that Anne's molester was experiencing the same hell we were all going through. But he never saw her screaming from nightmares, or had to hold her while she cried herself back to sleep. And he never had to go looking for her and find her hiding in the closet because she was afraid he would come back and hurt her again."

• "I wanted to be as far from my husband as possible when I found out he had molested Angela. He hurt my baby, and I never wanted to see him again. I hoped our going away would hurt him as much as he had hurt us."

Reality Check Number 10:
What Behaviors Are Typical During the Anger Stage of the Grief Process?

✔ Calling the investigators and telling them they aren't doing their jobs properly or quickly enough.

✔ Fighting with family members about everything.

✔ Trying to place blame on family members or others for what happened.

✔ Expecting the therapist to be angry *for* you, and to be able to quickly "fix the hurt."

✔ Threatening harm to the molester or his or her family.

✔ Going to the newspapers and demanding that the molester be jailed immediately.

Guilt and Depression

Depression is anger we feel toward others, but instead direct at ourselves. By the nature of their roles, parents can be the most guilt-ridden people in the world. Janet and Bill experienced tremendous guilt because they felt they had not protected their child from Mr. Webster. Janet felt her nurturing of Scott had left him too naive, and Bill felt he had not fulfilled his role as the family protector. After Janet's initial cry, she retreated to their bedroom to look at Scott's baby pictures. Bill went out and worked on the car. At dinner, they took special care to give Scott the biggest dessert. During the next few days, Bill took Scott out to buy an expensive fishing pole.

Other parents tell their reactions, based on their feelings of guilt or depression:

• "I would look at my daughter and sob. She was so beautiful and innocent. I just knew that I had done everything wrong in my parenting for this to have happened."

• "I wanted to take away all of the hurt for my son. I didn't want to talk to him about the abuse, I just wanted him to forget it and have fun. I took him to the circus, movies, roller skating, and everywhere I could think of, instead of trying to resume a normal routine. After putting him to bed at night, I would weep."

• "I couldn't eat or sleeep for days. I would think about what that man did to my child and feel so bad inside that I couldn't function. I lost several days of work because I couldn't concentrate, and I really wasn't in any shape to be of much help to Barbara when she needed me most."

• "My husband started drinking again and sometimes I didn't know where he was. I'd be cryin' and he'd be drinkin'. We were good for nobody."

• "I enrolled my son in an expensive private school. It cost more than we could afford, but I thought I was protecting him by taking him out of the public schools where he had been molested on the playground by an older child. It wasn't the right solution, but it seemed like it at the time."

Reality Check Number 11:
What Types of Behaviors Do the Feelings Of Guilt and Depression Produce?

Many times parents place the blame on themselves, feeling guilty for whatever has happened to their children. Depression follows because the molestation has already taken place and parents turn their anger at what has happened away from the molester and back on themselves. When people are angry with themselves and feel guilty, they might:

✔ Indulge in negative habits (smoking, drinking, eating, etc.) to excess.

✔ Withdraw from other family members or friends, either physically or by not communicating.

✔ Want to sleep a lot.

✔ Be unable to sleep.

✔ Experience other physical symptoms: headaches, upset stomach, vomiting, diarrhea, and so on.

✔ Cry more easily and more often than usual.

✔ Become absent-minded, forgetting everyday things because they are so preoccupied with the abuse and their guilt.

✔ Feel an urgency to do things as a family that they've been meaning to do but have not until now.

✔ Attempt to isolate the family from friends and extended family members.

✔ Doubt their ability to make appropriate decisions.

Bargaining

People often attempt to "bargain away" a molestation to try to quickly forget that it ever happened. They try to become overwhelmed with other activities, projects, or thoughts. "We must be all right, because we're too busy to think about what happened" is what they are unconsciously saying to themselves— and sometimes to each other. Unfortunately, families can get stuck in the bargaining stage as parents try to go back to their family's previous life-style. If you find yourself involved in bargaining and don't recognize what you're trying to do and what it's doing to you, complete healing within your family may never occur. It is not recommended that, instead, you sit at home and brood about this awful thing that has happened, but do make yourself admit that the molestation *did* happen, and that it *has* had effects on your family that can be adapted to but not erased.

In the bargaining stage, Janet and Bill felt they would be able to create enough activity within the family that Scott would forget what happened to him. On top of an already busy schedule, they tried to wedge in extra fishing trips, family outings, more movies, and generally more of everything.

Other parents have reacted in similar ways:

• "I didn't want my child to go to her group therapy sessions. I thought that she had talked enough about what had happened to her. I didn't want her to remember. I thought she could go on and forget it if she just tried to put it behind her and got busy with other things."

• "Shortly after the abuse was reported, I started thinking

about when we would be able to move to another town—far away from all of Heather's bad memories. I thought being somewhere different would make everything OK. Fortunately, the counselor convinced us it wouldn't, and we're all glad we stayed here."

• "I got rid of all of the pictures of my husband, thinking that Mandy would forget about the daddy who had molested her if she didn't see them."

Reality Check Number 12:
What Behaviors Are Common in the Bargaining Stage of the Grief Process?

If you try to fill your life with superficial activity to block the unpleasant thoughts about what has happened, you might realize you are:

✔ Resisting going to therapy by cancelling appointments because the therapist insists that the problem be discussed until your child and family members have resolved it for themselves.

✔ Being overly attentive to your molested child's presumed needs and wants, feeling that will erase or make up for what happened.

✔ Resisting discussion within the family of the abuse and the problems it has caused.

✔ Busying yourself in unnecessary activity so there is less time to think about what happened.

✔ Demanding that family members "tough it out" or show super-human displays of nonemotion, and labeling or minimizing your feelings about the abuse. (A father may think of himself as "a sissy" if he cries; the mother feels she is "hysterical" if she's upset. These labels can keep you from facing your underlying feelings.)

Acceptance

When family members have accepted that the sexual abuse occurred, have not minimized it, have not exaggerated it, and have dealt with it in a healthy manner—with the assistance of a professional therapist—they are at the stage of acceptance. It may take a few months or several years to reach this stage. Individual family members may reach acceptance at different times, depending partly on who molested your child and the type of molestation. When you are accepting, you have let go of preconceived ideas about child molesters and about yourself as a parent, and have worked to restructure your families into a different, yet productive, family unit.

By accepting the fact that they must go through various stages of the grief process, Janet and Bill and their children are working toward acceptance. Their stages (just as yours) may not occur in the *sequence* listed here, and just when they think they are beyond one stage, old feelings may come back to remind them that there is still work to be done with some phase they thought they had already passed through.

You may even skip a stage or two. That does not mean you are doing something wrong. If you do not feel a great deal of guilt, you may simply know that you had no logical way of preventing what happened. If you didn't feel the necessity to try to bargain, you are saying you are ready to work at dealing openly with the family hurt—not trying to get so busy that you can forget it.

These stages can actually be blessings. It is important that you recognize them for what they are, and allow yourself to feel them as they occur for you. For instance, when you feel angry, you can let yourself experience it without acting on it in an unhealthy way. You may feel as though you really want to physically hurt the molester, and acknowledge that feeling without actually doing anything harmful. Hit or kick a pillow or write letters you *won't* mail. Scream and cry in a place where you feel safe *and* where your child can't hear you. Work out in a health club. Take a brisk walk or a strenuous bike ride.

It is common for these stages to creep in unexpectedly and unpredictably. Recognize them as a normal response to your child's abuse. Take comfort in reminding yourself that these awful feelings will not stay with you forever, unless you deny their existence and refuse to work through them. They are unpleasant, but you *will* survive. See these stages as building blocks for your recovery and the healing of your family.

9

How to Help Your Child Cope, and How to Select and Work with a Therapist

THE time following the report of a molestation is understandably difficult for your child. It also places heavy responsibilities on you as a parent and as an adult to help your child. We often think of our children as "little adults." They are not. They are children, and have a right to have feelings and behaviors that would be unrealistic and unacceptable in an adult, but are understandable and permissible in a child. Although children have a right to have their own feelings about what has happened to them, they still tend to take cues from the adults they love about how to react. This places you in the position of having to walk the tightrope between making light of what has happened to your child, and overreacting to the point that your child feels like "permanently damaged goods."

If you step in and smother your child with attention and concern, saying repeatedly how awful it is that this horrible thing has happened, he or she will not believe in his or her own power of recovery.

Allison was a beautiful little girl molested by her older brother's friend. Because of early childhood illnesses, her father had always viewed her as especially fragile. When Allison reported she had been fondled by the older boy, her parents—particularly her father—were crushed. Her father began to be overprotective, supervising her contacts with children in the neighborhood and excessively limiting her outside activities. At bedtime, he would rock her and tell her that no one was ever going to hurt her again. As an eight-year-old, Allison was confused by her father's intense attention. Her mother had the good sense to convince him that his behaviors were becoming overwhelming to Allison, who seemed to be losing self-confidence because of his actions. Although his fears were normal and his intentions good, his behaviors were not productive. Therapy was needed to resolve his fears and redirect his actions.

Your major task is to provide an environment that your child feels is physically, psychologically, and emotionally safe. This will provide an atmosphere in which your child can progress successfully through the recovery process.

Be prepared for the behaviors (see chapter 4) that sometimes arise in children who have been sexually molested to continue, and even for new ones to develop, after the molestation has been divulged. A six-year-old who had no history of bedwetting began wetting the bed almost nightly after her abuse became known. Her parents did not say, "See what that awful person has done to you!" and reinforce their child's fear that she was a different and "bad" person after the abuse. Instead, they quietly changed the bedding and reassured her that it was OK, and would soon stop. In that supportive, "safe" environment, the problem soon ended.

Scott began having nightmares. He would knock on his parents' door during the night and say he'd had a bad dream. Often the dreams were somehow connected to his camping memories. Sometimes a bear was chasing him and trying to eat him. Or he would dream of falling into deep water, and not being able to swim to shore. Janet or Bill would hold him and calm him down. If he asked to sleep in their room for the rest of the night, they would help him spread his sleeping bag on the floor beside their bed. They could have forced him to go back to his room, feeling that he was taking advantage of the situation or that he would never be willing to go back on his own if they let him stay. Instead, they were there for him at a time when he needed them and, after a few weeks, the nightmares stopped, and he was comfortable in his own room again.

Following a molestation, a child may show behaviors that appear to be deliberately seductive. Often these are behaviors taught to him or her by the abuser and, because they pleased that person, the child is confused when others are repelled and view the actions as "sluttish" or "whore-like." Nine-year-old Betsy was observed at school rubbing the crotch of a younger child on the playground. A teacher, not recognizing the relationship between Betsy's behavior and the fact that she had been molested, reported her actions not as those of a victim but of a "little hussy."

An adult survivor of sexual abuse as a child remembers the feeling of *not* having a safe place to talk about her molestation, her bad dreams, and her fears. "My parents told me the sooner I forgot about my rape by a family friend, the better it would be. They couldn't cope with my nightmares. They told me I was being silly and to go back to sleep and the bad dreams would go away. They told me to put the past behind me and get on with my life. At ten, I really needed their help. I'm in therapy now—twenty years later—because the nightmares never went away."

Sexual molestation is being talked about more openly, and the vital importance of professional therapy for victims and their families is becoming an accepted fact. Thousands of adults who were victims as children are now joining support groups and seeking the therapy they should have had ten or twenty or even thirty years ago. For most of these victims, therapists specializing in sexual abuse counseling did not even exist when they needed them. Victims' stories of their frustrations and failures over the years, because of problems relating to their molestations that they were never able to work through, take away all doubt of how essential therapy is. Many of them did not identify their problems as being related to childhood abuse until they read about the patterns of failure that the abuse can set up, and recognized their own destructive behaviors.

It is important to get your child and your family into therapy as soon as possible. Studies have shown that the family is most receptive to help during the crisis/disclosure stage—right after the abuse has been discovered and/or reported to authorities. An especially effective counseling relationship can often be established at this time. One of the reasons therapy is particularly helpful and needed at this stage is because the family is working with legal and investigative teams where everything is black and white. Of necessity, judgments from these teams must be made about what happened. A therapist can help you work through your feelings in ways the other support systems can't. Therapy can be a very comfortable place for your child, and each family member, to take his or her worries and concerns.

The therapist may also be helpful by getting to know your child and becoming a potential expert witness if court proceedings follow. The therapist can offer a place of centeredness and support for your family.

Recognizing Your Need for Therapy

If you are in a fairly progressive section of the country, regarding social services, therapy will be strongly recommended for your child and your family. In some instances, particularly in cases of incest, families are even court-ordered to enter *and complete* a program of treatment. Many people prefer to think that they can care for their own emotional worries, but when your child has been sexually molested the stress the experience creates for family members really needs to be discussed with an objective, trained professional. Don't feel insulted by anyone's suggestion that you talk to a professional "family coach."

Selecting a Therapist

It is very important to your family's recovery that you work with a therapist specifically trained and practiced in dealing with families who have experienced a sexual molestation. This is a field requiring special expertise. Just as you wouldn't choose a foot doctor for an earache, it is very unlikely that someone with a general mental health background can work with you as effectively as a sexual abuse specialist. Therapists with special training *in addition to* their backgrounds as clinical social workers, licensed mental health experts (such as marriage and family therapists and psychologists), or psychiatrists should be able to provide the best help for your family.

Remember that you are the consumer—the customer. You have a right to ask questions and determine a therapist's suitability for your family's needs. In some communities you may not have the luxury of having many therapists to choose from, but—from those available—you should still try to select the one best suited to your family needs.

Reality Check Number 13:
What Questions Can Help You Decide If a Therapist Is Qualified to Help You and Your Family?

The types of questions you could ask, over the phone or in person, to help you select a therapist include:

✔ Where did you receive your specialized training?

✔ When were you trained?

It is important, at the postgraduate level, for the therapist to have received family therapy training from a qualified institute. Your therapist should have received workshop, seminar, or institute training in the areas of family counseling.

Sexual abuse treatment training is available in workshop sessions also. These workshops are created to teach therapists the causes, process, and resolution of sexual abuse-related problems. The therapist who has been to workshop sessions should be able to effectively apply the learned information to guiding your family through the currently recommended treatment process.

✔ How long have you worked in the field of sexual abuse counseling?

The field of sexual abuse treatment as a specialty is relatively new, within about the last ten years. Don't be surprised if a therapist has only been working specifically in this field for two or three years. The important thing is to have had specialized training in working with sexually abused children and their families.

✔ Approximately how many families or cases of sexual molestation have you worked with?

To be really experienced in this special area of treatment, a therapist should have worked with a few hundred or more cases. If you are living in a sparsely populated area where mental health services are not often used, a qualified therapist may have worked with fifty cases. Again, training is the key factor.

✔ Do you work with the entire family, or just the victim?

A therapist who has been specifically trained will want to work with your entire family through a significant portion of the treatment program. Though the exact process may vary, the therapist will probably want to see the parents (alone) first to find out how they are feeling about the molestation. During the same session or at an additional one the therapist will want to see the child alone. With young children, this time will be spent in play therapy; with older, in discussion. The therapist will schedule a session with all family members to assess how they view what happened to the victim and how each feels he or she was affected.

During the course of treatment, the therapist may request to see family members individually, in selected pairings, or the entire family together. At sessions, the therapist may request that you rearrange your seating, speak directly to a particular other family member, or rephrase your comments or questions to make them more clear. Your therapist may use a number of different ways to elicit honest feelings and to resolve differences between family members. There is no one "right" way.

✔ Do you frequently work with other agency professionals in sexual abuse cases?

It is important for the therapist to feel that the treatment of sexual abuse is a team effort. Discretion will be used in divulging confidential matters that do not directly apply to the sexual abuse; however, it is important for the therapist to work with the investigative team and connect with any other therapists working with your family, when it is appropriate.

✔ Are you familiar with the reasons for and the process of videotaping molested children?

The therapist should be familiar with the videotaping procedure (if it has not already been done during the investigative process), and should have access to the videotape of the investigation interview with your child. Most therapists understand the advantages of working with videotaping of the victim during the investigation, and of the victim or entire family during treatment, even though they may not have access to the equipment.

✔ What are the differences between fixated and regressed pedophiles?

The therapist's explanation should include a brief mention that fixation indicates the more acute type of problem in a child molester. A regressed pedophile's offense is often more situational (occurring when a particular situation made it possible, and not as part of a recurring pattern of behavior for that person) and his or her problem more easily treated. If the therapist cannot explain, it may indicate inadequate specialized sexual abuse training.

✔ Can you recommend some reading that might be helpful to me, my child, or my family?

A therapist should be able to recommend some books that would be helpful to you, and may also suggest articles.

✔ What experts have influenced your work?

Some of those currently recognized nationally as experts are Groth, Burgess, Sgroi, McGovern.

✔ Do you use psychological testing (either done by you or referred to other professionals) in your treatment program?

> Although it is not essential for the resolution
> of your child's trauma from the abuse, therapists
> often administer psychological testing or refer
> the victim and/or other family members for it.
> These tests can help validate the emotional
> effects of the abuse on the child, and are often
> requested for court evidence. The nonoffending
> parent, particularly in incest cases, also may be
> asked to take some psychological tests.

You do not have to know the "correct" answers to these
questions for the answers you receive to be helpful to you. Be
wary if you feel a therapist is not comfortable and conversant
about the subject of sexual abuse treatment. Not having ready
answers for these questions *might* indicate that a therapist feels
a generic mental health approach is sufficient in sexual abuse
treatment cases, too. Usually it is not. Qualified therapists will
be open to your questions and will not be defensive.

The reputation of the therapist you select is important. If the
professionals involved in the investigation have had specific
training in sexual abuse, ask whom they recommend. If they
have not had specific training, they may perceive the special
procedures and precautions taken by a specialized therapist as
unnecessary or foolish, and not recommend him or her. You'll
have to decide how much to rely on their recommendation.

If you are fortunate enough to have a choice, discuss with
your child whether he or she would prefer to work with a male
or female therapist.

Working Effectively with Your Therapist

The first priority of the therapist should be the continued
protection of your child. Try to work with a therapist who
wants to see that the molester is treated fairly, but who puts
your child's welfare *first*. A therapist with this emphasis helps

see that your child is protected by an even broader system of support than just your family.

Therapy is not like a coat of paint that can be brushed on your family by someone to make you all shiny and new. It takes effort on your part for the process to be truly helpful, and the changes have to come from within. The following suggestions will help you get the most out of your therapy sessions.

Reality Check Number 14:
What Should You Keep in Mind to Work Most Effectively with a Therapist?

When you begin your counseling with a therapist, it is important for you and your family members to keep in mind the following:

✔ You will have to be honest and open about your feelings about the molestation. Your feelings won't be judged as right or wrong, they will just be accepted as your reality.

✔ Your therapist will not "put a label" on you or your family members (such as stupid, hopeless, or crazy). He or she will work to assist you in improving your ways of communicating within the family, in order to resolve your feelings surrounding the abuse.

✔ You will need to be open to the idea that therapy could take three or 103 sessions. There is no magical formula that completes the family's healing in a predetermined length of time.

✔ You should be willing to sign a release of information form, authorizing your therapist to discuss appropriate information with other agencies when applicable to the court case. The therapist will honor the family's confidentiality during therapy process, but his or her observations about the apparent effects of the abuse on the child can be very helpful to the court proceedings.

✔ You need to accept that effective therapy is not always pleasant therapy. You may find yourself or some of your family members becoming upset during some sessions. Do not be afraid of the anger or sadness the therapist helps you express during your family's recovery. Don't let the temporary discomfort keep you from completing the treatment program.

✔ Not all communities can offer counseling without charge. Community mental health centers usually charge fees that vary according to income. The therapist who is most qualified to work with your family, however, may be in private practice. Health insurance will often pay a substantial part of the fees. Keep in mind that you want the most qualified person, wherever she or he may be. Be willing to invest financially in your family's healing, if that is necessary and possible.

Use the list you've just read to help you make a wise choice of the person to conduct your counseling. A good therapist can help you guide your responses to your child in ways that will help get rid of his or her fears—and yours as well.

10

Dealing with Your Family's Feelings of Guilt

GUILT is the result of telling yourself you've done something wrong, and feeling regret over it. It is usually associated with feeling responsible for another person's hurt. Janet and Bill experienced the feelings of guilt that are very common in the parents of a sexually molested child.

Guilt causes problems both *for* individual family members and *between* them. There is a reluctance to express feelings of guilt openly, for fear that other family members will see the expression as a sign of weakness. The tension and frustration from holding in true feelings can cause family members to isolate themselves from one another.

Bill and Janet were unknowingly expressing their feelings of guilt when they consistently gave Scott the largest dessert and bought him expensive gifts. This did not go unnoticed by the other children in the family. Beth and Brad were very aware that their parents were giving Scott special treatment. At seven, Beth grew resentful after just a few days of what she saw as her parent's seemingly making Scott "the favorite." Brad, seventeen, wondered what all the fuss was about.

As weeks went by, Beth and Brad found themselves giving in to all the special demands of the investigation and Scott's immediate needs. They silently resented the way all of this was disrupting their lives, but felt guilty about complaining because they realized what a bad time it was for Scott and their parents.

The children reacted to the situation in different ways. Beth started whining and complaining to get her parents' attention. She would cling to her mother whenever they went out. She began faking stomachaches, and asked to stay home from school on several occasions. She knew that when she was home during the day, she had her mother's undivided attention. Beth felt guilty about her actions, but they "worked." She got the attention she needed, even if it wasn't always favorable. Janet and Bill were so distracted by their involvement with the legal process that Beth's actions only annoyed and exhausted them. It did not occur to them until they began therapy to ask Beth directly how she was feeling about what had happened and about having so much attention focused on Scott.

Brad, never open about his feelings, withdrew from the family even more. He spent extra time with his friends, broke his curfew, and let his grades slip. His parents seemed to him to be unavailable, interested only in Scott at the moment. Brad told himself that his resentment of Scott was wrong, and he felt guilty. He was looking forward to going to college the next year, and needed his parents' help in deciding on a school. He was angry that they had no time to spend with him to help make the choice. Janet and Bill saw Brad's choice of a school as something they'd get to "just as soon as the immediate demands of Scott's problem were met."

These were normal responses for the brothers and sisters of an abuse victim, and for the parents. When they were able to talk about how they felt with their therapist, they were better able to understand and meet each other's needs.

If you let your feelings of guilt progress to the point where you become overwhelmed by what has happened to your child, they will cause you to become unresponsive to your child's needs. You may also add to your child's feeling of being damaged goods.

Parents talk about how they felt after becoming aware of the abuse:

• "After the abuse, my whole family fell apart. I didn't realize that I had always been the force holding it together. When all of my energies went to helping my abused child, the family couldn't keep going without my leadership. My daily routine changed, to focus on my Stephanie and her needs. That disrupted the routine of the whole family. I felt guilty about neglecting my other children's needs, yet at the same time I felt helpless to manage my life in a way that included them when Stephanie's needs put such heavy demands on my time."

• "Because I was a single parent, I felt I was spread painfully thin during the crisis time. My attentions were focused on helping the legal system punish my daughter's abuser. I felt guilty that I hadn't protected her from this man, and wanted to make up for what I felt I had neglected to do. In the process, I was trying to work and supervise my other child, who had been diagnosed as hyperactive and had a learning disability. But I knew he was not getting the attention and help he needed. It was a pretty rough time."

• "My husband molested our daughter, and the authorities told me that he must get out of our home or I couldn't keep custody of her. My husband and I had been married for seventeen years, and I was still in love with him. I wanted to believe he was telling the truth when he claimed he had never touched Jill. But what Jill said seemed to be true. At first, I resented her for telling what had happened. Then I felt guilty for being resentful, because I knew I had to protect her. I felt very torn between my loyalties to each of them. It was the worst time of my life."

• "When our only child was molested, I felt that there should have been some way I could have protected him. To cover my guilt, I began spending all of my free time with him, to the point of neglecting my wife—who was having real problems over what had happened, too. It nearly destroyed our marriage. At the time when we needed each other the most, I withdrew from her. I'm lucky that we had a good therapist to work with who helped me put things back in perspective."

Barbara Turner, the Child Protection Team member who was working with Scott and his family, referred them to Michael Phelps, who has a master's degree in social work and training and experience in child sexual abuse therapy. Michael knew it was typical for the family to be experiencing guilt and remorse over feelings arising out of the situation created by Scott's abuse. During his first interview with just Janet and Bill, he tried to determine how much their guilt was going to delay or prevent the healing of their hurt and Scott's.

As Michael spoke with Janet in the presence of her husband, he could see that she was examining her own ideas about what was expected of her in her role as a mother. He made a mental note to question her further about her feeling that she could have prevented the abuse. Her guilt was focused on blaming herself for the ways she allowed her children to become involved in activities outside of the family.

Bill's guilt was largely the result of feeling he somehow let Scott down, and for wanting the abuser to suffer some extreme punishment. Bill felt that expressing his anger toward Webster openly would be wrong, and he felt guilty for not being more compassionate toward another human being. Raised in a forgiving, Christian environment, Bill felt his thoughts were shameful.

When Michael interviewed Scott, he was pleased to see that, in spite of the abuse, Scott had maintained reasonably age-appropriate behaviors and emotions. Scott's guilt was mostly based on his feelings that somehow he must have attracted Mr. Webster's unwanted attentions by something he had done. Scott felt he *must* have done something wrong for the abuse to have happened to him.

As Michael spoke with Beth and Brad in the family sessions, he sensed that they held resentments toward their brother, but they felt it would be wrong to express them. He saw Beth hanging onto her mother and Brad sitting apart from the rest of the family. He saw everyone "polite-ing" each other to death, in an effort to avoid conflicts. He knew that the family did this because they did not want Scott to feel responsible for the uncomfortable feelings that had developed between family members since the abuse. There was a lot of tension in those early therapy sessions.

During therapy, Michael explained to the family that guilty feelings are very appropriate when someone has *intentionally* hurt someone else. As a matter of fact, it's an important sign of having a conscience. A conscience is necessary to distinguish between right and wrong and to make moral decisions. In the case of sexual offenders, it is important that they feel guilt and remorse over what they've done if they are to be able to benefit from treatment. In our society, people who are unable to feel guilt and express remorse are considered sociopaths. (Those are people who act out in socially unacceptable ways with no remorse, from used-car salesmen who knowingly misrepresent their products to guilt-free mass murderers.)

Michael went on to explain that *getting stuck* in guilty feelings prevents people from taking responsibility for making things different. He pointed out to Janet and Bill that giving Scott special favors was an attempt to make themselves feel less guilty. However, telling Scott that they would protect him was an act of responsibility. He went on to say that the family was also being responsible by coming to counseling and agreeing to accept Michael as a skilled coach to guide the family in communicating their feelings in acceptable and healing ways.

In the same way, you can let your therapist help you break free from unproductive guilt, and lead you and your family along the road toward healing.

11

Healing the Communication Process within Your Family

THE family stress caused by the molestation of your child can cause many problems. Fortunately, most of the problems can be worked through with the help of effective family communication. If the ways you have communicated in the past did not resolve conflicts effectively, or left you feeling isolated in your pain, this is the time to take advantage of an unpleasant situation and allow yourself to open up to the possibilities of new approaches to communication. You may have to work extra hard with your therapist to learn good communication skills as you strive to heal the family hurt, but it will be well worth your effort.

Fortunately, effective communication is something that *can* be learned, if people realize they have a problem and are open to trying new ways of working toward a solution.

Reality Check Number 15:
What Are Some Indications of Breakdowns in Family Communications?

Communication breakdowns between couples or family members are sometimes indicated by:

✔ Unpredictable flares of temper.

🖋   An increase of serious fights between family members.

🖋   Excessive amounts of television watching, reading, or sleeping.

🖋   An increased and/or excessive use of alcohol or drugs, leading to arguments.

🖋   A lack of time set aside for fun, for the parents as a couple or for the family as a group.

🖋   Excessive time spent away from home by a family member.

🖋   Erratic eating patterns with no (or fewer) shared family meals.

🖋   Family members' spending excessive time alone in their rooms.

🖋   Total avoidance of conflict in situations in which it would normally arise.

🖋   A family member's obsession with an activity that formerly was only of minor interest.

🖋   A change in sexual pattern and relationship between the couple.

🖋   Physical violence.

All families have arguments. It's how the arguments are resolved that makes the difference between whether resentments remain, or whether family members can go on effectively with their lives, even after something unpleasant has happened to them. Bickering among children in the family is normal and to be expected. And parents have their own unique set of couple-relationship patterns and challenges that come with being married or being part of a close relationship. Even in the healthiest families, problems are a part of life. Working toward the resolution of those problems is part of the commitment that people assume if they choose to continue relationships.

Most adults did not learn from their parents that it was a good thing to openly express their feelings. Older generations did not feel that way. Saying what you needed and how you felt was often associated with weakness—something to feel guilty about. Actually, it is a sign of strength when you can define your needs and state them to others. That's the only way they can respond sincerely, telling you whether they can easily do what you are asking or whether negotiation and compromise will be necessary. You can't expect others to magically know how you feel, even when you think you've made it very clear by your actions.

The old classic example of the strong man was John Wayne. Now perhaps it's Clint Eastwood or Arnold Schwarzenegger. How many times in their movies have you heard these macho stereotypes say, "I need your help," or "I'm feeling sad," to their heroines? Their roles portray them as possessing super-human self-sufficiency. They don't need anyone. It's ridiculous, yet it looks convincing on the screen; convincing enough that some men feel it is their duty to imitate those performances.

Women, too, have had some unrealistic role models. Don't forget the portrayals of women who smilingly take care of *everything* at home, without making "unreasonable" demands for any help from their spouses. Updated heroines now manage full-time demanding careers *and* busy families, and we still don't often hear, "I need more help with disciplining the children," or "Instead of playing golf on Saturdays, please help me with the grocery shopping."

Thank goodness people have begun to learn to change their styles of communicating, realizing that the old ways learned from their parents and other role models often don't work for them. Magazines are now full of good communication suggestions. Talk shows have opened up the sharing of human experiences that would have been considered too personal in the past. We've learned that it's OK to talk about what has happened to us and how it made us feel. In fact, it's healthy.

Bill and Janet considered themselves fairly open with each other. Yet prior to the disclosure made by Scott, they had had a few communication problems in their relationship. Janet sometimes felt that Bill was not able to discuss what appeared to be worrying him. Often she only knew he was upset by what he did around the house. He would busy himself with his boat or ham radio. It was frustrating for Janet that he didn't seem to want to express or share his feelings with her. Bill, whose father never talked about such things, saw Janet's questions about why he seemed upset as bothersome nagging. The verbal roadblocks he set up left Janet feeling there was no real resolution of the problem, even after they had tried to talk. Until their counseling began, this pattern continued in relation to the events following the molestation.

Although Bill angrily pounded the table the day he learned about Scott's experience, he immediately regained his composure. Janet, on the other hand, cried most of the day. And she was eager to discuss her feelings with Bill and to discuss with Scott how he felt about what had happened. Janet took the lead in communicating with Scott and the authorities. Bill withdrew to his boat. Janet felt abandoned by Bill at a time when she needed his support. When Janet asked Bill how he felt about someone molesting his son, Bill blew up. "How do you *think* I feel!" he said, and stomped out of the room.

The types of communication problems Janet and Bill had are common when two people must learn to negotiate the different ways they express feelings. The fact that Scott was molested only accentuated their already present communication difficulties.

Janet was very eager to seek the help of a therapist. Bill was resistant. He was frightened about revealing his thoughts and feelings. Suppose the therapist found out the awful things he had imagined doing to the offender? Suppose he was asked to "spill his guts"? What would happen then? He was the head of the family. What if he cried in front of his children? What kind of example would that be for them?

Bill's feelings are not unusual. He was afraid to show what he perceived as a weak part of himself during a time when he felt he needed to be the strongest family member. His other fear was that the therapist might think he was crazy. Going to a stranger with his family's problem meant that he would have to overcome some of those fears. That, in itself, was a scary proposition.

Initially Bill felt that the normal lives of their other children would only be needlessly interrupted if they had to become involved in the therapy sessions, too.

It's surprising how many parents do not even tell the other children in the family that their brother or sister has been molested. In wanting to protect the other children from hurt or alarm, some parents will go to great lengths to try to keep this information a secret. This is common, and it's a mistake. The other children will know that *something* is wrong. They may even fear that something *they* have done is upsetting the family. It is obviously easier to keep this information from children who are not living in the home, but they, too, need to be informed.

Even when children within the family are aware that something of a sexual nature has happened to their sister or brother, parents frequently will not go any further in explaining. And they forget how important it is to stress that they will provide protection to *all* their other children, too, to see that nothing similar happens to them.

Parents frequently resist bringing all the family members into therapy. They say that talking any more about the molestation will only serve to upset the other children in the family. This attitude prevents the other children from having a chance to work through their feelings and fears about the abuse with the help of a trained professional. Families with communication problems have much to gain by sitting down with a therapist and letting that person act as an impartial family communications coach. Though the abuse is the factor that brings them there together, often old unresolved conflicts that have lurked in the background for years can finally be worked through to everyone's benefit. Therapists often hear family members say to one another, "I never knew you felt that way," or "When you say that in the form of a request rather than a command, I can understand how you feel and it makes me willing to help you."

After the initial interviews with the various family members, Michael saw the Thompsons as a group. He took careful note of where each member sat in relation to the others, which family members talked to which other members, and what styles of communication were used.

During this meeting, Michael asked each family member how he or she wished to be helped by the counseling. Bill expressed an interest in clearing up any problems as soon as possible so that the family could get back "on track." Janet wanted to be sure there would be no long-term problems for Scott as a result of the molestation, and wanted the tension she felt between family members to go away. Scott wanted his Mom and Dad to stop "fighting." Beth thought she wanted her parents to pay some attention to her again. Brad didn't see why he had to be there at all, and felt too much was being made of what had happened.

Michael's job was to create a safe place for family members to express themselves. He could tell that Janet and Bill had had some difficulty communicating even before Scott's abuse was discovered. He felt this was a unique opportunity for the family members to learn to relate to each other more openly. One of his ultimate goals was to hear an unguarded discussion of how each member felt about the molestation and the way it had affected the family. As he explained to the family, there was no way to determine in advance how long the recovery process would take.

At the end of his first session with all of them, Michael asked if they felt the time with him had been helpful. He wanted this question to get them thinking about what they wanted to be different in their future communication patterns and what they felt had been accomplished in that direction.

During the sessions that followed, Michael asked Janet and Bill to sit next to each other, sometimes asked a family member to direct his or her comment to a specific other member, and often suggested that a comment be rephrased in non-blameful language. For example, after Bill's comment to Janet that "You make me feel guilty when I'm relaxing and you're on the phone calling some agency about what happened to Scott," Michael asked Bill to drop the "You make me," and say, instead, "I feel guilty." This was a way of asking Bill to be responsible for his own feelings.

When Beth blurted out, "You don't love me anymore!" to her parents, Michael explored with Beth what made her feel that way and then asked her to rephrase her feeling as "I miss doing the things we used to do together." This was something her parents could respond to without feeling defensive. People can respond in a more relaxed way when remarks don't accuse them of something.

Michael asked the family, between sessions, to do "homework." Janet and Bill were to have one night out together during the week, and special time was to be set aside for family activities. Soon Scott was able to discuss his feelings of being the "different" child in the family. He said he had always wanted to be like his older brother, because Brad was so cool. He was worried that Brad thought he was acting like a baby over what had happened to him. Brad had no idea that Scott admired him so much. With Michael's help, Brad was able to admit that he had felt isolated from the rest of the family and he promised to take Scott to a movie. Michael had told Brad that his help would be needed in the healing process because Brad was a role model for the other children.

Over the next few weeks, the family began to feel less

tension during and between the sessions. Janet and Bill began to relax, which made them more available to all of their children. Even Brad admitted to enjoying the family's Sunday dinners. Scott shared more play-time with his sister, and Beth's "stomachaches" went away.

The session arrived when Michael asked Scott to discuss Mr. Webster's actions. Janet was worried that Scott would feel too threatened in front of his brother and sister. Michael gently explained that it was important to discuss even difficult things with those close to you. As Scott explained what happened, how Mr. Webster approached him and how he felt about having someone he trusted do something so awful, the other family members were able to show their concern and love. Bill began to cry in front of his family, and didn't try to hide it. Michael explained that Bill was very normal to feel this way and that his tears were a way of expressing his caring for Scott. The children saw their father in a new light. He became a real person to them, not just a "father." Janet appreciated the tenderness that Bill was finally able to express. Beth and Brad were able to tell Scott they loved him and didn't feel that he was any different just because someone had touched him in improper ways. They told him they knew what happened wasn't his fault. The family left the session with a renewed sense of trust and togetherness.

Michael knew that this family, as all families, would have challenges to meet, but he felt they had really begun forming new communication habits that would help them in future difficulties. He began to see the family less frequently, with visits lessening to once a month. Eventually he felt the family no longer needed a coach, but, in his last session with them, made it clear that he was available if they needed him for future reality checks.

The counseling, which initially appeared to be a threatening experience for the family, had instead given them new skills in communicating their wants and needs to one another. The family members learned to trust one another in new and different ways, ways that eliminated the need for family secrets and hidden agendas. As Bill remarked to Michael on his way out of the door for the last time, "I was reluctant to come to counseling, but what it's done for our family is very helpful."

Later, at home, when a family member forgot to use the communication skills they had learned, a good-natured reminder put their discussions back on a productive course. They felt comfortable about calling Michael if they felt "stuck" on a problem.

The Thompsons' experience is not unusual. Remember that no matter how scary it may seem at first to talk with a professional—an objective "outsider"—the results can make the difference between getting on with your lives and staying resentful and hurt. Your child's recovery and that of your family are well worth the time, money and energies you will spend getting professional help.

12

What to Say to Extended Family Members, Friends, and Others

O NE of the challenges your family will face during this difficult time will be what to say to others about the molestation.

Obviously, if the molestation receives newspaper publicity, even though your child's name does not appear, many more people will be aware of what has happened than if it is handled quietly. Keep in mind that you do not *have to* respond to anyone's questions or comments (including those of representatives of newspapers or other media) regarding the situation if you do not choose to.

If there is no publicity or public awareness, it will be left almost completely to you to decide whom you will tell.

Janet and Bill had already been in contact with parents of the other boys in Scott's camping club and, as time went by, found comfort in discussing problems and feelings with these parents in addition to their therapist.

At first Janet and Bill felt they did not want to share knowledge of Scott's abuse with any family members other than Beth and Brad. Bill was an only child and his parents lived in a distant city. Janet's family lived closer, but not in the same town. She knew at some point she would have to tell her sister, but was especially reluctant to tell her parents.

The time came when they would soon all be together for a holiday dinner. Janet and Bill felt the subject of the abuse might come up in conversation with Beth or Brad at some time during the visit. Janet called her sister first, whose understanding and supportive attitude—and appreciation of being allowed to share the family's hurt—convinced Janet to tell her parents before they came to visit.

During a phone conversation, Janet mentioned to her mother—trying to sound as casual as possible—that Scott had told Bill of his club leader's inappropriate behaviors. She also assured her mother that Scott was being protected, that the information had been reported to the authorities, and that the whole family was receiving proper counseling.

Understandably, her mother's first reaction was shock. She regained her composure, and said she knew that these things were being talked about and handled differently these days than when her children were young, and she was glad they were getting help.

Then her mother surprised Janet by asking her *not* to tell her father. She said he had such violent reactions to hearing about child molesters that she was afraid he'd make a scene at the family dinner, demanding that the molester be castrated or saying something else that would upset Scott and everybody.

At first, Janet agreed. But after thinking about it she called her parents again and told her father about the molestation, saying she needed his help. She said she understood his strong feelings about molesters, but that it was very important for Scott that the molestation not be made into more of a stressful happening than it already was. Her father agreed not to express his anger and disgust for the molester in front of Scott or the other children.

It took obvious effort, but at the family dinner he carefully controlled his comments. The occasion was festive, undimmed by the shadow of the molestation.

The reactions you get from relatives and friends will be as different as those individuals are different.

Reality Check Number 16:
What Can You Say to Others about the Molestation?

To help make your conversations with others easier, keep the following in mind:

✔ The protection of your child's privacy, to the extent that it is reasonably possible, is very important.

✔ You don't "owe it" to anyone to explain *in detail* what happened, with the exception of investigative authorities and your therapist.

✔ Depending on his or her age, your child may have a right to know whom you have told about the molestation, or even to participate in the decision of who is told.

✔ You have the right to ask friends and relatives not to discuss with others what you tell them about what happened, to protect your child's privacy.

✔ Having responses already in mind can help you feel less uncomfortable when someone comments or asks about what happened. (Suggestions follow later on in this chapter.)

✔ It can be helpful to your child if you give him or her suggestions of responses to use if other people bring up the molestation. (Suggestions follow.)

✔ Very young children often talk about their abuse at inappropriate times or to inappropriate people. (Discussion of this follows.)

✔ If you have to be firm, abrupt, or even rude to get people to understand how important your child's privacy is, that's OK. Your child's welfare comes first.

Your child will probably feel embarrassed about the molestation. Initially, he or she may even feel responsible. With counseling, that unrealistic feeling of responsibility will go away. Let your child know with which relatives you will be discussing the subject, and even get his or her permission—if you feel that's appropriate. It is important to help maintain your child's sense of privacy. Only those people who have a reason to know need to be told.

Sometimes an extended family member is the first person to learn of the abuse, because that is the person to whom a child divulges what happened. If this is true in your situation, you may feel hurt that someone knew even before you. Don't feel defensive toward that person because your child chose to tell him or her instead of you. Understand that your child may have been trying to protect your feelings by disclosing to someone else. Your child may have felt that person could tell you, better than he or she felt able to, what happened, and in a less upsetting way. Instead, be grateful that a relative could be so close and caring that your child felt able to talk to that person, and that the relative felt open enough to come to you with this sensitive information. If your child is that comfortable with this relative, chances are that you are close to this person, too, and so will not feel resentment toward him or her.

Regardless of who the molester is, someone within the family or outside, if you are especially close to your extended family (mother, father, siblings, aunts, uncles, grandparents), chances are you will want to talk with them about your child's molestation and how it has affected the family. It is important to keep in mind how these relatives usually react to stressful situations. That is how they can be expected to react when they hear what has happened. As with friends, the reactions of relatives to news of the molestation will range from hysteria, obvious distress, sincere concern, embarrassment, horror, disgust, polite indifference, disinterest, or an unnecessary probing for all the intimate details.

If your relationship with your family is on a long-distance or rather cool basis, it is easier for you to delay relating or discussing the abuse when you first learn of it and may not be ready to share. If you know that relatives will react in blameful, critical, or totally unresponsive ways, you may not want to share the information with them unless it becomes absolutely necessary—or until you feel you can handle their negative reactions.

Responding to Others' Comments and Reactions

Family members and friends might already know what has happened from reading a newspaper report or by word of mouth. In some communities news travels quickly. People may approach you even before you have the opportunity to tell them. Or they may visit or phone to express sympathy or anger to your child, before you have even had a chance to discuss the situation with the necessary authorities.

Reactions could range from the extremes of "Your child's lying again!" to "I feel awful about what happened. News of the abuse has me so upset that I had to make a doctor's appointment because my ulcer started acting up again."

One mother reports that her daughter's grandparents were so upset after hearing about the abuse that they couldn't talk to her daughter without having their eyes fill with tears. She found herself having to comfort her husband's parents almost as much as her daughter, and it placed an additional emotional burden on her. Her seven-year-old daughter, Alyce, was confused by their reactions, and they made what happened seem all the more terrible to her. When the grandparents were included in one of the family's therapy sessions, they became much more able to cope with what had happened to Alyce.

People's reactions toward sexual molestation are so different that you can't expect them to react in ways that seem reasonable to you. Some extended family members and friends may experience, to a lesser extent, the same grief reactions that you do, because they care deeply about you and your child. Appreciate their concern, but continue to protect your child and his or her privacy, too. Remember that you can remain in control, and you can decide with whom and to what extent you wish to discuss the abuse. In some cases, people will speak only in whispers when they talk of the sexual abuse. They will refer to the victim with such phrases as "poor little Scott, who never had the chance to learn about sex in a normal way." Ask them, politely, not to behave this way in front of your child. It is important that you, as a parent, make it clear that because your child was sexually molested does not mean that he or she is "abnormal" or "ill" or "ruined for life."

Megan, age ten, had discussed her abuse with her best friend, Diane. Diane told her parents, who began to tell their friends and associates. In church one Sunday, Megan's mother overheard a stranger refer to her daughter as "the dear little Keller child who was raped." Unfortunately, you cannot be sure that word of your child's molestation will be kept within the family and extended family, or even within your circle of close friends. Megan's mother could, however, approach Diane's parents and request that they keep the information as quiet as possible to protect Megan's privacy. She did this in a nonaccusing way, and they agreed.

Special Problems in Incest Situations

In cases of incest, if a relative has divulged the information to you rather than having it come to you directly from your child, don't let the pain of what they tell you turn you against the person telling you about it. People who must convey this type of information to a parent are placed in an awful position. If you worry about whom else the person has talked to, when you still don't want anyone else to know, it is perfectly reasonable to ask, and then request that no one else be told right now. This will give you time to talk with your child and to have the report investigated, if you feel this is appropriate. Even then, you can request that the information not be shared with any other family members until you feel the time is right.

In these cases of sexual molestation of a child by a relative, entire families often split apart—taking sides over who's to blame, or whether it even happened. It is normal for the immediate family of the abuser not to want to believe what has happened. It is not uncommon for aunts to support their niece or nephew even when the child's mother (their sister) is disbelieving. Many families will disown the victim and the victim's parents when the parents speak out about their child's being abused by an uncle or cousin or grandfather.

Sadly, in some families, sexual abuse has become an accepted way of life and a part of routine family interactions. When the molest is reported in families such as this and authorities are brought in, the victim and parents may receive threats or be shunned by other family members. The relative who reports the abuse is thought of as a betrayer. In these dysfunctional families, it is common for family victims to be labeled "troublemakers," "liars," "sluts," "scheming little tramps," and other derogatory terms. Extended family members look on the disclosure of the abuse as telling "the family secret" to outsiders. In families where sexual abuse is common, some family members have a tendency to wonder what all the fuss is about when a molestation is revealed. They may feel they have grown up "just fine" even though they were victims of abuse as children, not recognizing the problem behaviors the abuse has caused throughout their lives. Chapter 14 discusses incest in more detail.

Reality Check Number 17:
What Types of Comments Can You Expect from
Others about the Molestation?

A few of the infinite variety of possible comments include:

✔ "We were so sad to hear about the horrible thing that happened to your child."

✔ "Don't you just want to kill the molester!"

✔ "What exactly did he do to your child?"

✔ "I don't know how I could live through my child being molested!"

✔ "Your poor child must be feeling really guilty."

✔ "Are you sure your child didn't make it up? Children have such vivid imaginations these days."

✔ "Why didn't you know it was happening?"

✔ "If it were my child, I'd just move away."

✔ "Don't worry. Kids get over things fast. In a couple of weeks she'll forget all about it."

You don't owe anyone an explanation. "I'd rather not talk about it" is an acceptable and appropriate response, if it expresses how you feel. Or simply, "It's been a very difficult time for all of us." Another generic response you may want to have ready is "I appreciate your concern." Or it may be easier to just nod as an acknowledgment of what someone says, without either indicating agreement or arguing.

Unless you feel that the person will be discreet, it is more important to protect your child's privacy than to give the person information, even if they request it. Remember that you don't have to tell anyone anything that you don't care to share.

Keep in mind that most people have very little factual knowledge about sexual abuse. Though they mean well, their comments are often based on the old myths about child molestation.

If you feel strong enough, this is your opportunity to do some educating, without divulging any specifics about your child's case.

For example, in response to the comment about your child feeling guilty, you could say that children *always* feel unnecessarily guilty in these cases until they are assured that they are not responsible in any way for what happened.

Being asked why you didn't know it was happening may really "push your buttons." Because as a parent you may quite naturally experience guilt over your child's hurt, you may react defensively. You really don't have to answer directly, you can say something such as "Parents do their best, but we're only human."

If people press for details beyond what you are willing to share, tell them that you would rather just keep things quiet, so you're not discussing the molestation except with authorities. "Because there are (or there may be) legal procedures pending, I'm not able to talk about it" will get most people to leave you alone.

Adults are the people most likely to say something directly to your child. You can instruct your child to respond to the most common comment, "I'm sorry about what happened to you," with a simple "Thank you." Tell your child that he or she doesn't *have to* respond to any comments or questions. If they feel cornered, saying "I'd rather not talk about it" or—if they don't feel comfortable saying that—"My mom and dad told me not to talk about it now" is OK. If other children comment or tease, your child might simply say, "It could happen to anyone."

Some children feel very comfortable talking about what happened with anybody. Young children, particularly, may want to tell the mail deliverer, check-out person at the grocery store, other children, and nearly anyone who will listen. If you feel your child is talking about the molestation inappropriately, or if that total openness makes you uncomfortable, you can explain that there are things you can talk about with family and close friends, but that other people may not understand. Let your child know that he or she can discuss the molestation openly at home, during counseling, or with authorities, just not in public places with people they don't know well.

Even if your child's comments to strangers seem inappropriate, don't make a scene about it at the time. If your young child knows that talking about the molest is another way of getting your attention, he or she may continue to talk about it. You can say, "Yes, that happened," if you feel it's absolutely necessary to make some comment to the person after your child says something, and then change the subject or walk away.

Don't confuse asking your child to limit whom he or she talks with about the abuse with "keeping the family secret." The first is a very acceptable request while the second is usually an unacceptable method of dealing with an unhealthy family situation. As long as all the *appropriate* people know what happened, people who can offer support and help your child and your family recover from the trauma, there is no reason why lots of others have to be aware of it.

Counseling also will help you feel less obligated to explain unnecessarily to others. Meanwhile, having answers ready and feeling you are in control of conversations on the subject will make you feel less helpless when uncomfortable situations arise.

Be comforted by the fact that it's a temporary situation. As time passes, the molestation will become less of a topic of conversation and will be less of a central focus in your lives. Then you won't be constantly faced with having to comment or respond to comments about it.

13

When Your Child—or You—Must Appear in Court

Whether the legal conclusion of your child's molestation is a criminal trial is pretty much out of your hands. Criminal trials represent the state's charging people with crimes against society, not with individuals bringing charges for wrongs done to them, as in civil trials.

Most states require social agencies (as well as professionals such as doctors, attorneys, teachers, counselors, and others) to report cases of child sexual molestation to law enforcement agencies. If it is felt that there is enough evidence to convict the molester, criminal charges will probably be filed against him or her. (See chapter 14 for information on *family* court, which will have jurisdiction in incest cases or when divorce, custody, or visitation disputes are factors.)

A preliminary hearing or a grand jury hearing could be the first court appearance required of your child, but it is unlikely he or she will have to appear. If either of these proceedings determines that there is probable cause to believe a criminal offense has been committed and the defendant is the person likely to have committed that offense, an indictment will be returned and a criminal trial date will be set.

Grand Jury Hearing

The prosecution (represented by the state attorney), if it chooses, may request a grand jury to review the evidence of a criminal act. Witnesses to the offense are called to testify before the grand jury and are subject to questioning by the state attorney and the grand jurors. (These jurors are selected by the same method used for calling other jurors.) In a grand jury proceeding, the defendant and his or her attorney do not participate in the proceedings and are not even present.

Preliminary Hearing

In some situations and some jurisdictions, a defendant has the right to an adversary preliminary hearing on the charges pending against him or her. A preliminary hearing is essentially a minitrial, held with a judge presiding and the defendant present. Witnesses are called to testify, and are subject to cross-examination by the defense attorney. The burden of proving probable cause is on the state.

Criminal Trial

When it has been determined that your child's case will go to trial, knowing what to expect is the best way you can prepare your child and yourself. Knowlege of what's involved during the legal proceedings that lead up to the trial and what is likely to take place in the courtroom will help make everything less frightening for your child.

During the time before the trial, your family will have an opportunity to begin the healing process. It can be hard to have to stir everything up again by going to trial. You may feel that your life will be disrupted all over again by what happened, just as things may be starting to get back to normal. Your initial reaction of wanting severe legal revenge against the molester may have mellowed into feelings of just wanting to get everything over with. You may feel frustrated that, once again, your energies will have to focus on the molestation.

Discuss your feelings with your therapist, if your family is still receiving counseling. If you are no longer going for regular therapy session, you may want to call and schedule a session or two to help you cope with the extra stresses of this trying time.

Depositions

If your child must go through a deposition, have the state attorney explain to you and to your child *in advance* what to expect. Usually individuals can be deposed (questioned) only once, unless new evidence is turned up between the deposition and the time of trial.

The people usually present at a deposition are the defense attorney, the prosecuting attorney, a court reporter, the witness who is testifying (your child), and a guardian ad litem, if one has been appointed for your child. The offender's attorney has the right to decide whether to allow the child's parent(s) to sit in during the deposition.

Often defense attorneys don't like to take the depositions of children. The state attorney you are working with may use this as a bargaining tool. If the molester is maintaining that he or she is innocent, the state attorney may insist that depositions of everyone else involved be taken *before* that of your child, making it clear that the state will not be as open to plea bargaining *after* your child has "been deposed" (has given recorded statements at a deposition). This will sometimes prompt better offers from the defense concerning the length of probation and treatment they are willing to accept in exchange for a guilty plea and no trial.

Videotaped Testimony

If your child can handle testifying in person, he or she will probably be asked to do so. Sometimes the emotional impact a jury gets from hearing in-person testimony does not come across on taped testimony. But if it is felt that a court appearance will traumatize your child too greatly, the state attorney may ask the judge's permission to use taped testimony, if your jurisdiction allows that procedure. Videotaped testimony is sometimes allowed in criminal trials, to prevent children from having to testify in person, but few judges are compelled, by law, to admit videotaped testimony.

Many courts are moving away from videotaped testimony for two reasons: some people still question whether such testimony meets constitutional requirements for giving the accused the opportunity to confront the accuser, and courts are making conscious adjustments to traditional testimony procedures to make them less traumatic for child victims.

Whether your child will testify in person or through videotaped testimony is often decided after court proceedings are begun. Procedures vary, but in Lee County, Florida, for instance, the judge, the defense attorney, and an assistant state attorney conduct a taped interview with the child. First the child is questioned by the state attorney and then cross-examined by the defense attorney. A judge is present to make rulings on evidence and points of law.

If videotaped testimony is used in place of courtroom testimony, your child will probably not have to make a court appearance at all. Exceptions would be if he or she is needed to identify the offender, or to dispute claims made by defense witnesses. In most cases, however, videotaping a child's testimony ends the child's involvement in the court case.

Parents are not usually allowed in the room or in sight of the child during interviews being videotaped. Not allowing you to be present during the taping is considered to be in the best interest of your child. Parents are often more emotional than their children. They sometimes feel compelled to prompt their children with comments such as, "But you told me that he . . .", "Didn't she . . . ?" "You told me that you said. . . ". Young children often revert to baby-talk and saying things such as, "Mommy, *you* tell them," when a parent is present. This can be true in depositions and court testimony, too. (Emotions run especially high in divorce custody cases involving an alleged abuse. In these cases, a family court is involved and decisions are made by a judge only, with no jury present. This is discussed more fully in chapter 14.)

Preparing Your Child for a Court Appearance

A court appearance can be temporarily frightening or even overwhelming for your child but, with some preparation, it should have no long-term ill effects. The better your child is prepared for what to expect, the easier it will be for him or her. The same is true for you.

The state attorney or Child Protection Team member will probably be the person who prepares your child for court. So that you will know what is said and can reinforce your child's understanding, you will probably want to go with them if they take your child to visit a courtroom (the same one the trial will be held in, if possible). In some jurisdictions, a brief meeting or a videotaped explanation may take the place of a visit to an actual courtroom. If the appropriate people or programs are not available to prepare your child, take the responsibility for doing it yourself.

If you plan to do this on your own, read through the following information carefully *before* you take your child to visit a courtroom. If you need any additional information to feel comfortable about accurately answering the questions your child may ask while you're there, try to get it before you go to the courtroom together, or take notes and get it right afterward.

Reality Check Number 18:
How Can You Help Prepare Your Child for a Court Appearance?

✔ A courtroom can intimidate even a secure adult. Think carefully about how *your child* is likely to feel during the trial.

✔ Be sure your child understands that the person who will be on trial *is the molester*. Your child may often hear the upcoming court appearance described to him or her as "your trial." Explain that the trial is *not* to decide what *your child* did wrong; that everyone knows he or she did *nothing* wrong. Tell your child that the trial is a way to help keep the molester from doing the same thing to other children.

✔ Talk with your child to find out what ideas he or she has about courtrooms, judges, or trials. Let your child freely express any fears or concerns. Ask questions such as: "What do you think it will be like when you go into the courtroom?" "Is there anything about a courtroom that makes you uncomfortable?" "What can I do—or ask someone else to do—that will make things easier for you?" "What do you think a judge does?" "Do you understand that no one can hurt you because of what you say here?"

✔ Really listen to what is said, and don't cut his or her comments short with reassurances. You can be more helpful if you are sure you understand first what ideas your child now holds. Many of them may be wrong.

✔ Few of us have much experience with the court system. If you find you haven't the specific knowledge needed to relieve your child's concerns, express those concerns to an authority who will talk with your child or who can give you information to pass on to your child.

✔ Take your child to an actual courtroom— the one where the trial will take place, if possible. It is probably better *not* to take your child to a courtroom with a case in progress, where shouting and theatrics could be occurring that may unnecessarily frighten your child. A good judge will not let that type of behavior go on in trials involving children, but that may be hard to explain to your child.

✔ Let your child sit in the judge's seat, jury box, in the witness chair, and wherever he or she might sit during the trial. As the room becomes more familiar it will feel less scary.

✔ Tell your child there will be a bailiff (sort of like a police officer) in the courtroom, and the abuser can't do anything to hurt him or her during the trial or afterward. Stress that it's a safe place for your child to be. Say there are many adults there to help get this difficult but necessary procedure over with as quickly as possible.

✔ Explain that a court reporter will be there to record what everyone says so there will be a permanent record. Show where that person will sit.

✔ Be sure your child meets—before the trial—the same state attorney who will be handling the prosecution's courtroom work. Ideally it will be the same person who has been involved in your case from the beginning, but if it is not, your child should meet the new person *before* the day of the trial.

✔ The prosecuting attorney should go over the questions he or she will be asking your child while in court. This is not "rehearsing the witness." It is a proper way of preparing your child, so don't let this make you uncomfortable. An attorney is negligent if he or she fails to properly prepare all of his or her witnesses for court.

✔ Your child should be prepared for the possibility that someone may say he or she is lying. Be sure he or she knows that *you*, and many of the other adults involved, believe that she or he *is* telling the truth. Let your child know that someone may say things such as, "You were told to say these things, weren't you?" or, "That didn't really happen, did it?" The defense attorney may ask the child, "Who told you what to say?" If your child is old enough, try to help him or her understand the difference between hearing the questions ahead of time and "being told what to say."

Keep in mind that the sexual abuse perpetrator usually has much to lose, personally and professionally, if found guilty. Defense tactics often emphasize discrediting the child's story, and, in the potentially intimidating courtroom setting, it is not always hard to do. A young child may not know the time of year or the day of the week when an incident occurred, particularly when the trial is taking place a year later. That's an age-appropriate lack of detail, but an attempt may be made to make a child's testimony appear unreliable in the eyes of the jury.

✔ If your child has already given a deposition, find out if the same attorney who questioned your child then will be defending the molester and questioning your child in the courtroom, so you can let your child know this.

✔ Point out where the defense attorney and the molester will sit in the courtroom. Explain to your child that the defense attorney will ask questions he or she probably won't like. Not because that person is mean; it's just part of the person's job.

✔ Stress the importance of trying to give the best possible answers to the questions, answers that tell exactly what happened. Children should be prepared for the fact that they may hear the abuser say things that are not true. They should be told that lying is wrong and that it's very important for them to think carefully about the answers they give, and to tell the truth, no matter what other people are doing.

✔ Your child should be told the types of questions the defense attorney is likely to ask, and should understand that it is that person's job to try to confuse him or her. This may keep him or her from "feeling dumb" when things are said in ways that are hard to understand. It should be explained that it is not necessary for your child to answer any questions he or she does not understand. Children should know, too, that they can ask to have a question asked again or said in another way to make it more clear before they answer, and that it's OK to take some time to think before answering.

✔ Let your child know it's OK if he or she can't remember the answer to *every* question asked. The memories of children concerning location, date, time, and sequence of events are often unclear. The state attorney will probably tell your child to say, "I don't remember," or, "I don't know," if the right answer can't be remembered, rather than guessing or making something up. The importance of trying to tell the truth should always be stressed.

✔ If anatomically correct dolls will be used in the courtroom to have your child show the jury what happened, your child should know this in advance.

✔ Depending on the age of your child, you may want to explain the jury as just a group of ordinary people who are there to help the judge decide what legal punishment the law says the molester should get. Say they will listen to what everyone says and then decide what should be done. Let your child know that the outcome of the trial is *not* his or her responsibility, and that the final decision may not seem fair.

Often children can view their initial videotaped interview just before the trial, and it offers a refresher of what they said back when the abuse was first reported. This visual form of review also has the advantage that, particularly for young children, they are interested enough in seeing themselves "on TV" to pay more attention when watching the tape being played. You may want to sit close to your child as he or she watches the tape, so you can offer reassurance if it appears to cause undue stress. If children have to sit through the reading of written transcripts of their original statements, they may not listen with as much interest, but they should be encouraged to concentrate.

If you are going to be called as a witness during the trial, you will not be allowed in the courtroom until it is time for your testimony. Your child should know ahead of time if you will not be there all of the time. If a Child Protection Team member is testifying, he or she may be allowed to stay in the courtroom afterward, to provide someone your child feels comfortable with and can make eye contact with if that will help make the situation less intimidating.

You may even *choose* not to be in the courtroom, if you feel you can't handle what will be said there. But it will usually have been several months, in the case of a criminal trial, and you will have had a chance to work through some of your feelings. If you just cannot stand being there, be sure you arrange with someone your child feels very comfortable with to be in the courtroom.

It is very possible that you and your family will get emotionally and psychologically prepared for a scheduled trial date and then the trial will be postponed. This may even happen more than once. (Chapter 7 covered how to cope with delays that are common in the court system.)

If the molester is found not guilty in a criminal trial, *that doesn't mean the abuse didn't happen*. And it doesn't mean your child lied. It simply means the molester was found not legally guilty. Be sure your child understands that he or she was not personally responsible for the outcome of the trial. This is particularly important when children are old enough to feel that the lack of a guilty verdict is somehow their fault. Other family members should be made to understand, too, that the child did the best he or she was capable of doing under the circumstances.

A not guilty verdict may be easier to understand if you realize that a molestation is often a very difficult crime for police to investigate and process. There is usually not what would be considered the traditional "crime scene." Unless there are (or were) visible physical indications of the abuse, there may be no evidence. Because most sexual abuse is nonviolent, involving no forceful physical contact, physical evidence is unusual. Few cases of abuse are witnessed by others. The trial becomes a case of one-on-one testimony: the child against the alleged abuser. Juries are faced with a child claiming that something wrong happened, and often with an adult claiming more articulately and more vehemently either that it didn't or that the child must have misunderstood what happened.

Most defense attorneys have learned that it's not in their best interests to try to make a young female child appear to have been a provocative tramp. It doesn't make sense. Things like that happened when cases of this type first began coming to trial, but they happen much less often now.

Understandably, juries are more comfortable when there are witnesses, evidence, and a crime scene. Instead, they get a child's words against those of a perpetrator who probably has a fresh haircut, "appropriately respectable" clothes, and a demeanor that his or her attorney has advised be adopted for the trial. Or the person is there, just being his or her normal self—a person not fitting the stereotype that so many people, including jury members, may think of as a child molester.

One CPT worker commented that if she didn't know the things she knows because of her job, she might be one of those jury members who would find it difficult to accept the testimony of a five-year-old that could send a man to prison for a capital felony for twenty-five years.

Fortunately, public awareness is growing that these seemingly bizarre things *do* happen, and much too frequently. As a result, juries are finding the stories of molested children easier to accept as the truth. They are also becoming more aware that the perpetrator must receive at least court-ordered therapy to break this deviant sexual pattern and for the protection of other children.

Scott was very nervous the day he testified, though it was helpful to have some of his friends from the camping club there going through the same thing. As they waited in the hall outside the courtroom to testify, some talked nervously about all kinds of things—not related to why they were there—while others were very silent.

There was obviously a mixture of triumph and sadness when Mr. Webster was found guilty of lewd and lascivious assault and sentenced to three to five years in prison followed by probation.

Scott's main reaction seemed to be relief that the trial was over. He was taking sailing lessons and seemed anxious to get on with his busy life and put the molestation behind him. Michael felt that Scott had recovered remarkably, and that interactions between the Thompson family members were better than before the therapy.

Janet and Bill were pleased and relieved that Scott was happy most of the time now. They also felt some satisfaction that the person who had been entrusted with the care of their son, and who had so hurtfully betrayed the trust of Scott and the other boys, had been punished by the legal system. They knew, though, that even if the trial had turned out differently, they would have been just as sure they had done the right thing by reporting the abuse to authorities.

If the trial of your child's molester does not end in a guilty verdict, try not to let any defeat or despair you may feel be too apparent to your child. Instead, praise your child for doing something you know was very difficult to do. Tell your child what he or she did was important and that something good was accomplished, even if the molester wasn't sentenced. The molester now knows that it's not possible to go on doing bad things to children without having it reported to the authorities.

Whatever the outcome, know that you made the right decision when you reported the abuse, and continue with your family's recovery.

14

When the Molestation Is Incest

I F the person who behaved in a sexually unacceptable way with your child is a member of your legal or social family, all of you face additional problems, problems that can permanently destroy the caring relationships that at one time probably existed.

With the wide variety of living arrangements that are common in our society, the former definition of incest has been broadened to include more molester/child relationships. The old use of the term incest was thought by most people to mean sexual intercourse between people who are so closely related that their marriage is illegal or forbidden by custom, such as a sexual relationship between a father and daughter. Now the molestation is generally considered an incestuous one when the molester of your child lives in your home, is related to you by blood, or is related to you by marriage. Depending on the life-style of the child's family, sexual abuse by others might also be considered incest.

The following examples would be classified as incestuous relationships by most experts in the field of sexual abuse:

Mary Ann's boyfriend had not moved into her home, but she felt that even though they were not married or officially living together, they shared a commitment. He often stayed overnight with her. When her daughter disclosed to her that

Kevin had been coming into her bedroom late at night trying to fondle her, Mary Ann realized he was attempting to have an incestuous relationship with her daughter.

Grandpa Jim had taken a special liking to his grandson Pete. He would invite Pete to stay over at his house. One day seven-year-old Pete reported to his parents that his grandfather had been routinely rubbing his penis, explaining that this was a way to help Pete relax before falling asleep at night.

A father was appalled to learn that his wife was using their seven-year-old daughter as part of the sexually oriented ritualistic acts of a cult she had joined.

Andrew's mom felt very protective of her five-year-old son. The two went everywhere and did everything together. They even showered together. She began to ask Andrew to wash her breasts and vaginal area when they were in the shower.

Uncle Keith described himself as a family man and often asked his nieces over to play in his swimming pool. Sometimes he would joke about having everyone swim without their swimsuits. Now and then he would get one of his nieces alone and ask her to show him her breasts.

Because families sometimes establish and pass on patterns of abuse, and because molesters—without treatment—seldom change, keep in mind that the uncle or brother-in-law or sister who abused you, or attempted to abuse you, is very likely to try to abuse your children. Don't assume that just because the person is older he or she is now "safe."

Just as sexual abuse does not have to include sexual intercourse to be a molestation, an abuse by a person related to the child in ways detailed above does not have to include sexual intercourse to be incest. It is important to be aware that incest, in the majority of cases, does *not* involve intercourse.

If your child has been molested by your spouse, date, or someone with whom you have a sexual relationship, as the protecting parent you have the responsibility and right to:

- Report the molestation to your local child welfare agency and/or to the police or sheriff's department.

- Demand at least a temporary end to all contact and visitations between the molester and your child.
- Obtain the necessary court orders to enforce this.
- Accept nothing short of complete protection for your child.
- Express the anger you feel in appropriate ways. You do not have to be pleasant to the molester, if you do not feel that way.

It is most imperative that the molester leave your home, if he or she has been living there, so your child can feel safe and be under as little stress as possible. In many states nonoffending parents do not have a choice in whether the offender leaves the home; it is mandatory.

If—against all advice to the contrary—the molester remains in your home or has free access to your child, it is very likely that your child has been or will be ordered by the court to live in a protective setting offering emergency shelter until the situation is legally resolved. This may be in the home of a relative, a state-licensed private home (foster home), or a group facility for children. If so, a case worker from the social service agency that requested such placement must visit your child in that residence on a mandated schedule.

Even if the state attorney decides not to follow through with criminal charges, the social service agency has other protective procedures available to them, if they feel your child is not safe in your home. They may petition for temporary custody of your child if they feel the child was neglected or that improper supervision was the reason for the molestation.

If a situation has arisen in which your child has been put into the care of another, try to imagine your child's feelings about being taken away from you. She or he is separated from the very person support is needed from the most right now—you.

If your child has been placed in a setting with other children going through similar situations, he or she may be hearing horror stories about what has happened to other children or other families. Children often wonder where they will end up living, and may be very fearful of being placed somewhere permanently, away from you. They may think that either the abuser or you or themselves—or all of you—may be put in jail.

Children in this situation are in the awful position of not knowing what the next day holds for them, and often imagining the worst. They begin to regret ever having told what happened to them. Sometimes their stories start to change. They may feel they can survive the abuse easier than they can survive not knowing what is going to happen to them and their families. If children change their stories at this point, it does not usually mean that what was said originally was untrue. It is more likely an indicator that they simply cannot cope with what they are going through, feel responsible for the confusion that is probably taking place, and are attempting to "make things better."

If *you* add to this isolation and uncertainty by accusing your child of trying to break up the family by making the incest known; if you place the blame for what happened on her or him; or if you threaten scary consequences ("What do you think we're going to eat if you get your daddy sent to jail?") you are taking the blame from where it belongs and placing it on a child who is already confused and frightened and desperately in need of your support, not your anger and threats.

You may be in the frightening position of seeing *your* future as just as uncertain as your child's. If the person accused is the primary source of income for you, the child, and possibly other children or relatives, you may see this situation as tearing your whole world apart. It is easy and common not to want to believe a small child's stories of what happened when believing can have such devastating results. But you must *believe and support your child.*

Realize that your child is probably feeling very confused about what happened. Usually the abuse is gradually introduced in a setting which was initially one of affection, caring, loving, and closeness. The child may still have *good* feelings about the abuser, too, because the relationship was, in some ways, seen by the child as nurturing. Yet it is vital that you constantly keep in mind that *children do not seduce adults*. When these caring relationships go beyond acceptable limits, it is never the fault of the child and it is always harmful to the child's normal psychological and sexual development, unless professional help is received after the abuse.

You may feel you could never forgive the molester for what has happened. Yet permanent loss of the close (and initially acceptable) relationship your child built with that person may be even more devastating to the child than what has happened to him or her. If the molester will admit to what happened, will accept full responsibility for it, will feel true remorse, will work toward helping family members take their rightful roles, and will help your child develop the self-esteem needed to operate as a functioning person, you and the child's molester may be able to pull the family back together. Your family may even become better than it ever was before.

Pressures bear down hard upon families in which incest has occurred, both internal and external. Your internal pressures come from the natural resistance to believing that this sort of thing has actually happened between two people you love.

When a stepfather is involved, the mother of the child often blames and condemns herself. One woman remembers feeling, "I've picked the *second* wrong husband. But I don't want my family to fall apart *again*." Her loyalties were torn between her child and her husband. There's no way of knowing for sure how you would feel until it happens. You may be willing to stick by your husband and see that he gets help, or you may feel as though you want to kill him.

Another woman reported how worthless she felt. "All I could think of was that I'd married a baby-raper, and that I must be not only stupid but a bad person."

Feelings of this type might make it hard for you to react at all rationally. It can be especially difficult to believe your child in these cases. Reports tell of mothers who, when they were told what had happened, responded with anger and accusations to their children such as "We're going to take you to the doctor right now and prove this is bullshit!"

External pressure may come from many sources: extended family members, friends, acquaintances, and nearly everyone you come in contact with who is aware of the situation. Be prepared for the revulsion most people feel at even the thought of incest.

And be prepared to have some family members demand that you not seek (or stop using) legal and professional help because you'll "ruin the family name" or "tear the family apart." Family members may find it particularly difficult to accept that one of their own is even capable of doing what is being reported. Aside from the convenient blindness that love often produces, they may unconsciously see it as a direct reflection on them when someone in their family is accused of incest. Or they may feel that the abuse was "no big deal," especially if sexual abuse is a common and accepted way of relating to one another sexually within their family.

The anger felt by both close and extended family members after the revelation of incest can take several forms: withdrawal from contact, blaming and threatening, or taking sides. If the molester denies what happened, relatives may begin choosing up sides in deciding who is telling the truth about what happened. Brothers and sisters of the victim can become anxious about their continued safety, and may act out in harmful ways such as temper outbursts, depression, destruction of property, running away, or exhibiting jealousy. All of the attention paid to the molested child may cause resentment from other children in the family.

Pressure can even be exerted by well-meaning "helpers" in the community. One woman reports that when she took her daughter's information about the incest to her clergyman, she was asked to keep this problem within the family and told that she should not report it to authorities, but should pray about it.

Adults who were incest victims as children report the great

disappointment and sadness they felt when their parents wanted them to hide "the secret." When such secrets are not discussed in an open manner, the effort it takes to hold back the truth creates great anxiety and depression within the family. If you were an incest victim as a child, you may find yourself accepting what happened to your child as almost "normal" and may place pressure on your child to accept what you had to accept as a child. "If I lived through it, my daughter can, too" is a sadly common response. Ignore these feelings, and seek the help for your child that he or she so badly needs.

When incest goes unreported, the problems that crop up later in the family can be severe, not only for the victim but also for other family members. It is very difficult for a couple, when one has been the molester, to have a healthy, open relationship, basically because the trust between the two has been shattered. Rebuilding it can be a long and difficult process.

Revealing the truth offers more hope for restructuring your family than trying to hide "the family secret." Seeking and responding to professional help provides your family with the best chance to become a supportive, functional unit—either again or for the first time.

For this to happen, all members must be willing to look at the roles they played in a family situation that somehow got out of control. You must all be willing to say, "Yes, our family has a real problem. But we're willing to work on it because we want to help our child grow up to be a healthy and productive adult. And we feel we can achieve this best as a healthy family unit." And you must be willing to work together toward changes that will allow your family to become one that "works."

As the nonoffending parent, you must also be willing to look closely at how your behaviors helped lead to what happened. This is in no way saying that you necessarily realized what the results of your behaviors would eventually be. Yet the nonoffending parent sometimes finds herself or himself watching a situation that slowly becomes incestuous and somehow seems impossible to stop. Clues about what is happening may include such things as someone focusing an unusual amount of attention on your child, your child's acting more attached to or more afraid of a given person, or your child's behaving in unusual ways. (Physical and behavioral indicators of abuse are discussed in chapter 4.) Parents sometimes feel overwhelmed by complicated circumstances and feel helpless. When one feels helpless to make something bad change, it seems easier to pretend nothing is happening. The incestuous relationship may even make the family *seem* to run smoother. Cases of violent sexual abuse of children are rare, so the child may *appear* not to be upset by what is happening.

When you are in a family where your boyfriend, husband, girlfriend or wife has sexually molested your child, you experience a feeling of great loss. You may find that your loyalties are torn. It is not unusual to hear the nonoffender say, "I don't know what or whom to believe."

Nonoffending mothers, in particular, often face financial and emotional losses at a time when they feel least able to support themselves in either area. Many times mothers will refuse to believe or will consciously minimize their child's molestation because they are frozen by their fears of having to support the family alone. Frequently the molester has been the family disciplinarian, also, and the prospect of rearing children without the traditional help of the husband or male authority figure is overwhelming to some women. These fears are understandable, yet they should not prevent you from protecting your child, reporting the abuse, and seeking treatment.

One mother explains, "The pain of what I experienced was almost indescribable. When I first heard that my husband had sexually molested our little girl, I was devastated. I went to my minister, who said that in order for the family to be healed, I must report the abuse. I became very angry. I had wanted my minister 'to make it all go away.' I thought that if my husband became religious, the responsibility for the abuse and for the family's healing would be put on someone else's shoulders. My minister said that part of the healing process was to bring the incest out into the open. He guided me to a therapist who knew how to work with sexual abuse within families. I eventually realized, with the help of both my minister and therapist, that I had done the right thing for my child, myself, and my husband by reporting the abuse."

Case studies show that successsful completion of a program of treatment is much more likely in cases in which the legal system steps in and assists the family. It is a rare family that, having reached this state of disrepair, can guide its own rebuilding. Professional help is as needed here as in any molestation.

Some incest cases never become involved in criminal court actions. If you work with a family court judge who believes in the family, and feels that yours is one that can be rebuilt effectively, he or she may issue court orders and instructions more geared toward healing than punishing. Many judges feel that incest is not an isolated happening, but is an indicator of more far-reaching family problems than will be solved by putting the abuser in prison. In these cases, when the abuser admits to what has happened and expresses a willingness to get counseling, the authorities may concentrate on efforts to help the family restructure and reunite rather than "seeing that justice is done," in the old frontier use of the term. Counseling then becomes an opportunity for the family to experience success, a much more productive process.

In areas fortunate enough to have child protection services and sexual abuse treatment programs, these agencies are being increasingly staffed by and recognized as competent, credible professionals who can give objective input, even though their main goal remains the protection of the child. These specially trained experts are in a unique position of being able to educate the family about what needs to be done to help the child, the family, *and* the offender.

If the alleged abuser continues to deny the charges and refuses to leave the home in spite of the child's claims, the child may be declared the temporary "dependent" of a social service agency with the proper legal authority. To do this, the agency must usually only establish a "preponderance of evidence"— enough to indicate that the abuse *probably* took place—rather than evidence "beyond a reasonable doubt," as in criminal cases. If your child's dependency is established through juvenile court, the social service agency can then keep the child in protective custody, insist that your family take part in a sexual abuse treatment program, if one is available in your area, or put your family under the supervision of the agency.

If you or the alleged molester contests the dependency ruling (claiming it is unfair, unnecessary, or whatever), lawyers must become involved. When this happens, the same delays and complications that arise in criminal cases can arise in your case.

If the charges of child sexual abuse against your spouse are part of a divorce or a custody or visitation dispute, you may face special prejudices, even among the professionals you come in contact with. This prejudice can be so strong that in spite of proof that, for instance, the father/husband or mother/wife was physically and sexually abusive toward the spouse during the marriage, and displays other characteristics known to be common among child abusers, the agency may dismiss your claims "because this is a custody dispute" and they assume all such claims are just made-up stories to discredit your marriage partner. In some cases, this happens even when the child describes the sexual abuse in detail, because some authorities assume that—as the disgruntled spouse—you have "put the child up to it."

If your lawyer urges you to compromise because "this will be a hard case to prove," think of the welfare of your child. Is any compromise acceptable? Do you want him or her living in fear of having to visit a molesting parent? If you feel your attorney does not understand the seriousness of the situation or is unsympathetic to your child's needs, do everything possible to obtain a different attorney. The compromises and agreements your attorney accepts will be legally binding. Keep your child's welfare your most important goal.

Even if you bring in a well-qualified expert to help substantiate your claim, the expert may be viewed as a "hired gun" or one of the pseudoexperts whose testimony can be bought to match the buyer's courtroom needs. You may also find yourself in a position in which your spouse has brought in a *real* "hired gun," to assure the court that your claims are unfounded. Until uniform standards are defined for "qualified experts" in the fairly new field of child sexual abuse, these problems will continue to arise.

It is recommended that the court judgment or order following testimony alleging a sexual abuse contain a written finding of the nature and extent of the abuse. If this is not done, you and the child may face years of the abuser's attempts to extend visitations or obtain custody, insisting that "nothing was ever proved."

The only acceptable solution in incest cases is for the abuser to admit the abuse, enter into appropriate therapy, and relinquish visitation rights until the therapists of the abuser and the child feel that appropriate contact can be resumed.

Be prepared to be involved in therapy for a long time. Most families, when initially hearing this information, resist the idea of a lengthy treatment program. They attempt to suppress the pain they feel about the abuse, and a quick therapy "cure-all" *appears* to be the ideal solution. They want something that will let them "get it over with" and get on with their lives.

Families who experience incest have multiple problems that often began in each partner's early experiences. It takes time to accept and apply different ways of living old family roles. Trust and communication issues have to be resolved. Consequently, courts routinely *order* families to undergo therapy, because the dropout rate among families receiving treatment under *voluntary* agreements is high when they experience the normal anxieties and fears that can arise during therapy.

"When they told me therapy would last at least twelve months and possibly much longer, I wondered why it had to take so long. I didn't think our family had that much to talk about," says a nonoffending mother. "I just thought everyone connected with the case wanted to punish us. It took a long time for my husband and me to see that therapy was our only chance to make things different. We were involved in treatment for over two years, and sometimes when we need reinforcement of some of the things we learned, we still go back to the therapist to talk."

"During the first few months," an incest victim explains, "I didn't want to say anything in therapy. I figured I'd created enough problems between my parents, and I didn't want to stir things up anymore than they already were. After a while, I figured out that I was not responsible for what happened, but I *was* responsible for my getting better. I got more comfortable, too. At first I was scared that my therapist would be judging me. It felt good to feel accepted instead."

A molester says, "Every time I would come up with an answer about why I molested my cousin, my therapist would have another question. Before I started in treatment, I thought the therapist would give me the answers. It took a long time for me to understand what happened to me as a child and see how that affected what I did as an adult. Shoot, I must have spent weeks arguing with my therapist that he should cure me. What a waste of time, of my time and his! I've been in this program a year and a half, and when I'm through I'm still going to come back from time to time. I don't feel I'll ever molest again, but I know I sure have a lot of personal growth that isn't finished."

Families of incest fear what will happen to them as individuals and as a unit as they work through the therapy process. That's normal. The child fears the loss of his or her parents' love. The parents fear loss of love from each other and from the child. Other children in the family may feel the family will break apart and they will be abandoned.

It takes great courage on the part of all family members as they begin their journey down this very special recovery path. To say that it will be easy would be misleading. Trust your inner strengths. They will help you face your fears and discover the strength that lies within you and can be shared with those you love.

15

You Know Your Family Is Getting Better When . . .

IT had been a year since Scott disclosed his abuse to his father. As Janet and Bill relaxed over coffee one night they talked about their family's experience. It had been a long year, and they had been abruptly introduced to many new aspects of life with which they had to cope.

Before Scott's molestation, Janet and Bill had never given much thought to their community's human service agencies or judicial system. They had somehow felt that the police investigators, child welfare workers, and therapists were there mainly for "other people"—people less fortunate than themselves. Their only, previous experience with the court system had been with a minor traffic violation. The molestation forced them to look closely at how our society protects children and works to meet their needs.

Bill and Janet had been naive about the length of time everything would take. They had imagined that Scott's offender would be arrested and jailed immediately after their report was filed. It was so apparent to them that Webster was guilty that they had assumed the investigation and trial would move very quickly.

Had it not been for the Child Protection Team worker's strong recommendation that the whole family seek counseling, they probably would not have realized how necessary it was to

their recovery. They would have struggled with their unresolved feelings and hurt, not knowing how to work through the
stages of their grief and becoming more isolated from each
other rather than growing closer.

They remembered their last session with Michael. He had
asked how they were now spending their time with one
another, and how their communications were different from
when the counseling began. As they thought about it, the
differences surprised them. The changes had happened gradually, but they were pleased with the progress they could share
with Michael.

Many of the positive things Janet and Bill observed about
their family are reflected in the following Reality Check,
offered to help you know when *your* family has experienced
significant healing.

Reality Check Number 19:
How Can You Tell If Your Family Is Getting Better?

You can feel good about your family's healing
when:

✔   Your child's behaviors resulting from the
abuse (bedwetting, excessive masturbation, poor
school performance, and so forth, see list in
chapter 4) have diminished or stopped.

✔   Thoughts surrounding the abuse do not
take up most of your time.

✔   There is less social isolation between family
members and between your family and outsiders.

✔   Family members are able to say what they
want in their relationships with each other, in a
nonblameful way. (See chapter 11 on communication.)

✔ Your family's routine has become fairly predictable once again.

✔ Your molested child and your other children behave in ways appropriate for their ages. If your eight-year-old is now playing more with friends her age rather than wanting to do "older things" such as always helping around the house, that's progress. Interest in age-appropriate toys may come back or become active for the first time. A teenage girl may get involved in after-school activities rather than just reading or listening to music alone.

✔ You and your mate are able to spend time with just each other and not talk about the abuse.

✔ You no longer think of everything in terms of how it might affect the child who was abused, but instead consider all your children equally.

✔ You have let go of your blame and anger at the molester. You will never forget what has happened to your child, and at times you may feel angry or blameful, but the focus of your life is not on how betrayed, resentful, and hostile you feel toward the molester and the world in general.

Remember, it was important to use your anger in a constructive way in the beginning. If you still feel some anger, don't deny it, because through expressing it appropriately, you will be better able to eventually let go of the feeling. (Review chapter 8 if you need help with this.)

✔ You have established "family time" (dinner, a special activity or outing, or an evening together periodically) during which you simply try to enjoy each other's company.

✔ You and your children have discussed a plan of action for your children if they are approached by someone inappropriately in the future. There are many excellent books, for children of all age levels, with prevention information, and your library should have some of them. You may find these very helpful.

It's important that your children know they can say "no" to an adult or authority figure when their body is involved. They need to know their bodies are their private property, and when someone approaches them in a way that makes them feel funny, they do not need to feel guilty about saying "no" and telling another adult what has happened.

✔ You are reasonably cautious, but not overly protective, in decisions about the outside activities in which you allow your abused child and your other children to participate.

✔ You can see relief and happiness in each other's faces. Family members seem less burdened and family interactions are less strained.

Your family's recovery time depends on so many different factors. If the molester was a family member, the abuse extended over a long period of time, or the molester denies that it happened, your recovery process may take longer than if your child was molested one time by a stranger who admitted the molestation and was sentenced. If the molester was not prosecuted, it may take you more therapy sessions to work through your anger. If the molester was tried and found innocent, that, too, stirs up anger that may be hard to resolve. If you find that the support systems in your community are inadequate, it will take extra effort on your part to work through your feelings of frustration and blame. This places a heavier burden on you and your family to seek every appropriate source to help heal the family hurt.

Janet and Bill were grateful for working through their hurt because they now communicate with each other and their children more effectively. The unfortunate experience resulted in Scott's confirming that his parents were a safe place to take his concerns, and he would be believed and protected. He also was assured that he was not responsible for his molestation or the problems it caused for his family, and that because he was sexually molested by a male did not mean that he was a homosexual. Beth and Brad knew that their parents would be there for them, too, if something they couldn't handle alone happened at some future time.

The molestation is something the Thompsons will never forget. Scott will always remember that an older authority figure wanted him to do sexual things that made him feel awful. His parents can't take that away. The molestation happened. Janet and Bill had never experienced that type of sorrow before, and *they* will never forget that it happened, either. Scott's brother and sister will never forget the child welfare worker and police officer coming to their house or the weeks of turmoil that followed.

One of the healthiest steps you can take is to recognize that it is unrealistic to believe that you can make your family just as it was before the abuse. This can never happen. Your family will be different—maybe even better. But no family is ever the same.

In working through your family's hurt, remember you do not need to be alone. As painful as it seems at the time, seek the help of skilled professionals. Others have survived the experience and come out healthier and stronger. You, too, can take what is initially a devastating happening and accomplish positive things as a result of that experience.

With your continued love and support, your child can have a good life. And with therapy, your family can have a life where the molestation takes its proper place in your past, and the future holds bright promises.

Glossary

THIS mini-dictionary is offered to help make you more familiar and comfortable with some of the words you will read in this book and hear as you work with authorities and therapists. The definitions given are intentionally not highly technical, but offer what we hope are the most workable explanations for the words as you read them here. The definitions are those commonly accepted, but you may also hear variations.

ABUSER: Used here interchangeably with molester, perpetrator, and defendant, to mean a person believed or known to have sexually molested a child.

ACT OUT: To behave in disruptive or nonproductive ways.

ADDRESS: Acknowledge that a situation exists and agree to talk about it.

ADMISSIBLE: Acceptable as evidence in a court of law. This varies by jurisdiction.

ADVOCACY: Active support of a person, cause, idea, or policy.

ADVOCATE: To speak on behalf of or to help protect the rights of. Here we speak mainly of child advocates.

AGE APPROPRIATE: Psychological or physical developments that fall within what is considered "normal" for a given age range.

ALLEGATION: An accusation or charge (of sexual abuse) made by one person against another.

ALLEGE: To claim or declare that something is true.

ANATOMICALLY CORRECT: Something (usually a doll or drawing) that fairly accurately depicts the human body. Often used with children so they can point to or somehow show what was done to them, particularly when they don't have the necessary vocabulary to do so, or when they are reluctant to speak.

ARRAIGNMENT: A court appearance before a judge by an accused person to hear the charges being made against him or her.

ASSAULT: An unlawful attempt or threat to injure another person physically.

BARGAINING: (As a stage of the grief process) Believing that involving one's self or one's family with activities and diversions will minimize or stop the hurt feelings surrounding the molestation.

BELIEF SYSTEM: The set of values and ideas associated with forming a person's perception of the world and how it functions, or "should" function.

CENTEREDNESS: A feeling or attitude that conveys a sense of personal balance and an inner peace.

CHILD PROTECTION TEAM: A crisis-oriented group from one or more professional disciplines, which intervenes when it is believed a child has been abused or molested. It may be an established local agency that consults with and works with child advocacy groups in the community. Known by various names including: Advocacy Team, Advocacy Center, Sexual Assault Team, Children's Crisis Unit. This service is not available in every community.

COERCE: To force to act or think in a given way through threats, pressure, or intimidation.

COERCION: The act of coercing (see coerce).

COERCIVE: Characterized by coercion (see coercion and coerce).

CONTEST: (As an action) To legally dispute or disagree with an allegation or judgment, and to seek to have it changed.

COPE: To work at or strive toward overcoming stressful conditions or situations; to overcome difficulties with success.

DEFENDANT: The person in a court action charged with having committed an unlawful act against another person, or a crime against society.

DEMAND FOR DISCOVERY: The right of the defendant's lawyer to request and examine all evidence to be presented in court against that person.

DEPENDENCY: A legal condition established to protect a child's welfare, in which the child becomes temporarily a dependent of the state and subject to a state agency's supervision.

DEPOSITION: A sworn statement by the principals in a case or a witness, taken by the opposing attorney and recorded by a court reporter, before the case comes to trial.

DISCLOSURE: A child's first statement (or that of a witness) that sexual abuse has occurred.

DOCKET: The calendar or schedule of court cases and when they will be heard by the judge to whom they have been assigned.

DYSFUNCTIONAL: Not meeting the needs of those involved. In a family it means having unresolved problems that prevent the family unit from working in the ways that are in the best interests of all the family members.

ELICIT: To obtain from someone or bring out; usually pertains to facts or that person's feelings.

ENVIRONMENT: The circumstances or conditions that surround a person and affect or influence his or her growth and development.

ESTRANGEMENT: The act, process, or result of becoming unsympathetic or hostile to the needs and desires of another.

EXTENDED FAMILY: Family including not just a couple and their children but also grandparents, aunts, uncles, cousins, in-laws, etc.

FAMILIAL: Pertaining to the family. Sometimes a custom passed on in a family.

"FAMILY SECRET:" Something happening within the family that is recognized as not acceptable to others and that family members are encouraged not to discuss with anyone—often not even with each other.

FELONY: A crime considered more serious than others (called misdemeanors); category of manslaughter, murder, and rape.

FIXATED: A type of sexual offender who seeks out children as the primary source of sexual gratification.

FUNCTIONING: Operating in such a way that the needs of all of those involved (as in a family) are adequately met.

GENITALIA: The organs of reproduction. In males: the penis, testicles, and prostate. In females: the vulva, vagina, uterus (womb), ovaries (egg area), and fallopian tubes (path between ovaries and uterus).

GENITALS: Usually used to refer to external (outside of the body) reproductive organs.

GUARDIAN AD LITEM: A person assigned by the court to protect the interests of a child.

HEALING PROCESS: The steps toward feeling better, overcoming, and recovering from the individual and family hurt (caused by a molestation).

HIDDEN AGENDA: An individual's unspoken intentions.

HYMEN: The membrane covering the entrance to the vagina. It can be torn during the first intercourse or insertion of an object into the vagina.

IMPACT: The result or effect one thing has upon another.

INCEST: Sexual molestation of a child by someone closely related by blood, related by marriage, or by someone in a social relationship where he or she could be broadly defined as "family."

INCESTUOUS: Pertaining to incest.

INDICTMENT: (Pronounced in-dight-ment) A formal accusation that someone has committed a particular crime.

INNATE: An essential characteristic of something, or something known by thought rather than through experience.

ISSUES: Concerns held by people (family members) regarding an occurrence that has had an affect on them (the molestation).

JURISDICTION: The right to make an authoritative ruling about a given matter, and also the range of territory over which a set of laws, controls, or authority applies.

LASCIVIOUS: Something that excites sexual desires (see lewd).

LET GO OF: To give up unproductive behaviors or previously held feelings, such as resentment, anger, or depression.

LEWD: Commonly thought of as lustful or indecent.

MAGISTRATE: A person with the authority to administer and enforce laws.

MANDATE: (noun) An enforceable command or instruction, usually issued by the court or an agency with legal authority.

MANDATE: (verb) To require that some command or instruction be carried out.

MOLEST: (noun) The name given to what happened: the molest. Interchangeable with molestation.

MOLESTATION: Involving or even asking children to engage in any sexual activity. This can include inappropriate touching (while the child is clothed or unclothed), exposure to pornographic materials, acts of bestiality, coercing sexual acts between children, or performing indecent sexual acts in the presence of a child.

MOLESTER: The person committing the act of molestation (used interchangeably here with abuser, perpetrator, and defendant).

MORAL: Conforming to established concepts of what is right and wrong.

NONOFFENDING PARENT: The parent who did not knowingly participate in the sexual molestation of his or her child.

NORMS: Standard models or patterns (of behavior or development) regarded as typical for a specific group.

PERPETRATOR: Used here to indicate the person committing a molestation (used interchangeably with abuser, molester, and defendant).

PLAINTIFF: The person claiming to have been harmed by the defendant in a court of law.

"POLITE-ING:"　Being excessively polite to avoid bringing up or facing a problem that exists between two or more individuals.

PROBABLE CAUSE:　The likelihood that something happened, but without legally conclusive evidence to prove that it did.

PROSECUTING ATTORNEY:　(see State attorney).

PROSECUTOR:　(see State attorney).

"PUSH YOUR BUTTONS:"　Do something to intentionally trigger a sure (or excessive) reaction to what is done.

REALITY:　What individuals experience internally as happening to them. A person's reality may or may not be based in fact.

"REALITY CHECK:"　A means of checking what is perceived with established norms (see Norms) to determine how one's perceptions compare. Not offered in this book to show you that your experience, feelings, or behaviors are "wrong," but to offer current information, to share with you what others experienced in similar situations, or to suggest productive ways of working through a situation.

REGRESSED:　Usually refers here to a molester who, under stress, reverts to molesting. Also means anything that goes back to a less reasoned and usually worse form of behavior, even more juvenile or more socially unacceptable. A "regressed pedophile" is usually considered one who will be more willing and likely to respond to treatment in a setting not requiring confinement.

RESOLUTION:　The lessening or ending of an undesirable condition or situation.

RESOLVE: To make a firm decision about, or to find a satisfying solution to, or bring to a successful conclusion.

SABOTAGE: To put up roadblocks against a desired result; an action to hinder or defeat what you claim to want to accomplish.

SELF-RATIONALE: The reasoning (excuses, explanations, etc.) individuals use to justify to themselves something they have done.

SIBLING: The brother or sister of the person being discussed.

SIGNIFICANT OTHER: Someone who plays an important role in another person's life.

SOCIOPATH: Person who behaves in ways not acceptable to society, with no feelings of guilt or remorse. Someone who does not conform to society's definitions of what is right and wrong.

SOCIOPATHIC: Indicating the attitude of a sociopath.

STATE ATTORNEY: The legal representative of the state in cases considered crimes (unlawful acts committed against society) such as sexual abuse, rape, murder, etc. Depending on the jurisdiction, also known as prosecuting attorney, district attorney (D.A.), county attorney, city attorney, state prosecutor.

SURVIVOR: Someone who has gone through a very trying experience (here a molestation). Sometimes a complimentary term for someone who has successfully overcome many problems.

THERAPIST: A specialist in conducting counseling, most frequently used here to refer to someone specifically trained to work with sexually abused children and their families.

THERAPY: The treatment of pyschological problems (related to the molestation).

TRAUMA: Severe emotional disruption or shock caused by an outside occurrence, such as a molestation.

TRAUMATIC: Something that causes trauma.

TRAUMATIZE: To cause a trauma to happen, or to be traumatized by an occurrence.

TRUTH (AS IN "YOUR CHILD'S TRUTH"):   An individual's interpretation of the world and what is happening in it.

VAGINA: The canal in females leading from the outside of the body to the cervix (the entrance) of the uterus (the womb where babies develop).

VAGINAL: Pertaining to the vagina (see vagina).

VALID: Sound, effective, based on a correct assumption.

VULVA: The outer lip-like surface at the opening to the vagina.

WARRANT: A written order for someone's arrest.

WORK THROUGH: To recognize that a problem exists, work to find an acceptable and satisfying way to solve it and, finally, to feel that the problem is no longer troublesome.

Index

About the Authors

KATHRYN B. HAGANS (who has changed her name back to Kathryn Brohl since the first printing of this book) is author of two other trauma recovery books: *Working With Traumatized Children: A Handbook for Healing* and *Pockets of Craziness: Examining Suspected Incest*. Ms. Brohl has trained mental health professionals in Australia, Canada, and throughout the United States. A licensed marriage and family therapist, she currently has a therapy and consulting practice in Miami, Florida.

JOYCE CASE is a freelance writer based in the mountains of Jasper, Georgia, and served on the board of directors of Concerned Citizens for Sexually Abused Children of Lee County, Florida, before relocating.

Reality Checks Notes